RELYUHCS

The Boys I Turned Into Men

A Poetic Memoir of Love, Longing, and Becoming

First edition

ISBN: 979-8-218-72271-5

Cover art by Gina Alm
Editing by Jessie Raymond

This book was professionally typeset on Reedsy.
Find out more at reedsy.com

To Cookie -
Thank you for always believing in me.
& wherever life has taken you, I hope you are smiling.
I will never forget how much about love you taught me.

.

Prologue

January 2025 -

There is an entity, something virtuous about this affair, a certain echelon of power that comes with it. Human connection is an unsurpassed decadence in life, a fundamental principle in cognizant existence. Who you love, who loves you, immensely elucidates the itinerary of your life. Love ultimately is the crystallization of your essence. An earthly beauty arises with the transmutation of a boy turning into a man. Even more alluring is the nourishment in knowing that your endeavor personified the venture. As they mutated into men, they simultaneously sculpted me into a woman.

The impending is an ode to the most intrinsic, prominent men in my life. Without the ascendancy of these men, I wouldn't be the woman I am today, despite a life of indeterminable miscalculations, a person I am proud of. I could chronicle an isolated novel about each of them and what they meant to me, but I find that the composition is unrivaled when put together. Without one, there would not be another.

Each one of them served a distinctive and quintessential purpose in my life. To say I loved one more or less than the others would not be fact. They exemplify each something unrepeatable. I treasured them with staggering contrast.

I began to delve through the catacomb of my heart, in search of what remained buried alive fearing the inescapable. The heart is a mesmerizing paradox, shattering time and time again, yet a fragmented heart never abstains from pulsating. The heart, the heart isn't delicate. It is designed to be destroyed unquestionably, to emerge more valorous… Mine, beating firmly with the remnants left behind by each of them.

I ask that you read with care and compassion, for I am only revealing my side of the story. These are a collection of my writings from 2011 to 2023. It's a devotion to each relationship, how each one shattered me, building me into the writer I am today. I will tell you everything, but how much of everything do you want to know? I have been torn repeatedly about how to compose this novel. How much power do words have? How differently these words would translate if written by Y, N, X, or G? It's a mix of power, love, sex, heartbreak, chaos, vicious honesty, and brilliance. It's writing in blood, feeling the mercy, as the ink traces the paper. It's an ode to how pivotal these men were in composing me. In turn, how I turned them into the men they are today. This isn't a novel; it is art.

And to all the women that have loved and will love them after me –
Most of you will live a life not even worth mentioning.
One day, you will die.
One day, the last person to remember you will die.
You will be forgotten.
My art, my words, this book will live forever.
I made them eternal.
You're welcome.

Y

17 years old

He has had a vast impact on the confidence I have today.
He was the first boy I ever took the time to write about.
He was the first I wanted to write about.

Y.1

I will see him today.

   How can I be held responsible for my actions?

   He makes me feel important; I want to feel this way forever.

We were introduced by friends a few weeks ago. I can't get him out of my head. I want him. I can admit that I want Y. We found ourselves innocently hanging out in our newly formed group of friends over the weekend.

There is something captivating about this boy.

Y.2

He has never said a mean thing about my appearance. He sees me when I am ugly. Everyone is sort of ugly when you think about it. I put almost no effort into how I look. Does he try? Do boys try to look good for girls? His lustrous dark skin, full lips, and large brown eyes sit symmetrically on his round, fleshy face. He stands a little less than 6 feet, his body composed of perfect, lean, sculpted muscle. He walks in an assertive way. His right foot leads, with his chin pointed loosely to the sky, and his left foot follows. His smile, though, that's what I like the most. He smiles so widely that his entire face transforms completely as his white, straight teeth beam to onlookers. A contagious smile. I like the way he looks. His textured curly short hair and his small ears complement the baby in his face; he has yet to outgrow them. He must like the way I look because, naturally, you are attracted to people you find attractive. When he does take the time to remark on the way I carry myself, it's always positive. Before I met him, I had no concept of what I looked like. I never found myself beautiful, but surely, I don't regard myself as unattractive, occasionally ugly, yes, but not unattractive. I don't know how to wear makeup, and I never do my hair. People tell me I am beautiful, but I don't always see it. I skipped school to smoke pot and play violin. I think I am too skinny, and my boobs are too small. Being a teenager is hard. Three times he has told me I am beautiful. I figure it must be true. Why else would he say it?

Y.3

He is always so sure of himself. He knows what he wants from life. How to get it. He can't see anything but his goals. He works hard. He makes sacrifices. If he is scared, he doesn't show it. He is fearless. He is confident. He wants to be the best basketball player. He is doing everything in his power to make it happen. He is unstoppable. Whatever he has in his blood, I want to have it, too.

Y.4

It's been two months since we first met. It's our senior year of high school and we have been regularly spending time together...

I can't stop smiling.

We often get so high from smoking the baby pink glass bong in the back seat of our friend's car. We have started to develop running gags amongst ourselves. We have forged a collection of small moments that we revisit playfully throughout the day.

I straddle him innocently while we laugh until our bellies hurt. My low-rise, dark denim Hollister jeans are tight on my thighs, pushing up against his white athletic shorts, as we laugh. I am trying to teach him how to put in eyedrops, intended to conceal that we have been smoking pot. I sit on top of him, pulling his eyelids apart, both crying from laughing so hard with the number of failed attempts. It is the closest physically we have ever really been to each other. I feel this force, an energy, psychologically pulling me towards him. I can smell the scent of his satin, dark skin through his cologne. He kept blinking just moments before the drops hit his dark brown eyes. His eyelashes blocked the drops, sending a river of what looked like tears down his cheeks.

When we had finally accomplished this task, we both were catching our breath from how violently we were laughing.

Moments like this, creating these small memories, revisiting them through a dialect only we understand—teenage affection.

It's cashhhhhhhhhhhhed.

Y.5

It's always my idea. He regularly says I'm crazy for thinking the way I do. I can't help it. I have a natural longing for adventure. It is his eager curiosity that pursues him to follow me.

We got drunk last night on Grey Goose vodka and stole our best friend's parents' white shiny golf cart. It was right there, just begging to be played with, waiting in the garage with the keys already in the ignition. I climbed in, turned the key slowly, and heard the motor awaken and come to life. I stared at him with my green, pear-colored eyes and smiled deliberately. "Please come with me, Y. It will be fun. Don't be boring. Pleeeease." I flirtatiously teased him until he finally gave in to my kittenish persuasion.

I pressed my right bare foot as hard as I could onto the gas pedal, driving it recklessly down their long, one-mile, winding driveway in the middle of that humid summer night. The light from the stars guided me, and the oak trees that lined the pavement helped me navigate as we drove off. A mixture of laughter and screaming came from him as he begged me to slow down. It took not even five minutes before I crashed the golf cart into the road sign, denting the metal post. I swerved hastily to avoid tipping us over, pressing instinctively again on the gas. He grabbed the wheel suddenly, jolting the cart, stopping only inches away from us, heading face first into the neighborhood pond, nearly destroying all the fun.

I wasn't allowed to drive it after that.

We laughed for hours this morning.
He was along for the ride, my accomplice.

Y.6

I wish I could read his mind.
   To know what he thinks of me.
   I wonder, could I handle the truth?
   I wish he could read my mind.
   To know the reality, I feel but can't say.

Y.7

It's riveting to watch him learn how to impress girls, to talk to them, to attract them, to play their games. I don't think he cared much for female attention until lately. Perhaps, it's the first time he is receiving it. I should warn him, navigating the female psyche is a suicide mission. It's enticing to watch him try on his own. Too stubborn to admit he is a virgin, as if it means anything to anyone. It's annoying to witness him with other girls. He starts to act like an idiot, trying to excite them. He plays stupid while teasing them. I watch with envy.

Y.8

I really don't know how our relationship started.
Was it stolen glances, secret smiles, and soft touches?
Laughter perhaps.
Maybe we just needed to feel alive for a moment?
We emerge as inseparable
With nothing to worry about until college starts,
Except when I will see him next, and if I should use my fake ID to buy us alcohol.

Y.9

He is blissfully naïve to the fact that I write about him.
   I will forge him into an illuminating, multifaceted poem or something.
   I think he would be gratified by the notion.
   The background on his iPhone is a picture of himself, a humble individual.
   As most would find that to be distasteful,
   I admire the illumination he has for his conviction.
   That's why I write about him, you know, because I commend him.

Y.10

I wish he would forget something in my car so he would have to come back for it later.

Y.11

Senior Year Spring Break:

My best friend has invited me to come with her to the Atlantis resort in the Bahamas.
   We will spend a week at the resort, in an island paradise.
   Everyone is coming, all our friends.
   Y will be there.

What happens in the Bahamas stays in the Bahamas.
Except when the five of us all got completely naked in the shower. That, you remember.

Y.12

He is the first person to ignite such desire in me. It's an instinct. He is triggering something primal in me. I am devoted to having him. The feelings are so complex. I often can't process them. I have never longed for someone so powerfully, and these feelings are tied so closely to my ego. I ceaselessly anticipate, with titillation, seeing him again.

The beauty of his body is the essence of his soul. I daydream about fucking him. Adapting this fantasy, my mind is incoherent all day and all night. It's becoming as close to an obsession as I have ever had, as if I will fail myself if I can't induce him to want me, to like me.

For the record.
I don't fail.

Y. 13

I absorbed stars from his skin
   Fell asleep digesting the constellations
   Memorizing the galaxies in his eyes
   Enchanted by the diabolical
   Inflamed by his cosmic love

Y.14

Pros list:

1. Ambitious
2. Aggressively determined
3. Purposeful life
4. Relentless – He won't stop until he gets what he wants
5. Has the ability to see the bigger picture - makes sacrifices because of it

I find these qualities most alluring.

Cons list:

1. I see a lot of myself in him

Inarguably terrifying.

Y.15

I don't feel like I need to try to make him like me; he would see right through me anyway. The last six months, he has examined me. He can predict what I will do with such certainty, the vicinity of reading my mind. I am existing in my own little hippie, pot-smoking, violin-playing world, and he is finding a place there. For the last few months, that world has been perfect, with him.

We are, without decoration, a casual conversation about the weather.

Y.16

The idea of dying doesn't scare me.
　　But his death?
　　This is my prevailing fear.
　　To be without him?
　　The world needs him more than it needs me.

I got stung by a bee today.
　　It died.
　　I can't trust him to taste me.
　　It's too dangerous.

Y.17

I pine from him the unfeasible-

I wish,
I wish,
I WISH,

I wish he would pledge not to conceal himself when he is sad. It's mindlessly distorted that we laugh together, but he cries alone. Do I even really know him?

Y. 18

We went on a walk this morning after waking up together. Like every weekend prior, we customarily sleep together in the guest room, at the end of the upstairs hallway, of our best friend's house. The green room. We wake up naked.

The air was tepid, and the sun was shimmering, splashing luminous glitter rays upon us. It was one of those summer mornings that you wish you could endure for an eternity. You can't help it. You crave the way the sun diffuses on your skin when you first step out of the door, encompassed with the fragrance of crisp, fresh-cut grass. A June summer day.

We belly-laughed recapping the shenanigans from the night before. I flourish joyously for the humor of the morning after a night of live music, cheap alcohol, and laughter. We walked the property for hours and talked until our friends finally woke. Our frivolous and lighthearted conversations mean more to me than anyone knows.

Y.19

Today, we were slumped next to the pool when he told me he feels like I need to be taken care of. In some capacity, I agree. Just this week, I got suspended from school for skipping a few weeks' worth of gym classes to smoke pot. Whoops. I think he often feels the ponderous liability of watching over me. I am out of control. I spend all my time doing teenage nonsense, but most recently, it has gotten out of hand.

I find it vaguely gratifying, all things considered, that he would worry this much about me.

"You need to calm down. People are worried about you. I am worried about you."

"I am fine, I am just having fun," I said, brushing him off.

"I don't know what I would do if anything happened to you."

Y. 20

Secretly, I keep him as my favorite incomplete wish.
  I think he knows.
  I think everyone knows how we feel about each other.
  It's exquisite.
  He makes me ecstatic.

Y. 21

I saw him and all my best friends graduate from high school today.
Poised so intentionally in his tailored black suit,
His face recently shaved. His curls distended, like a droplet framing his
head.
The men's choir sang.
His voice stood out, penetrating the audience, singing so regally,
beaming through the performance.
A gentle reminder of how adorable he is
His melody more hypnotic than the others.

Y.22

I had assembled in our college town for the summer. I was obligated to attend summer classes. I craved the emptiness of our town during the summer months. It couldn't have come at a better time. Two weeks ago, I procured pills from a stranger at a music festival. Days later, I found myself waking up in the hospital. Y witnessed the whole exploit, which remains the most embarrassing display of recklessness I've ever executed. Why did I do it? I became stationary to anything and everything. Life in general exhausted me. Drugs seemed like the rebuttal.

Present day – I highly advocate for an almost overdose. It will keep you from ever touching drugs again.

Now, I have school again, something to preoccupy my mind with. I am good at school. I adopted a stray cat that is illegally living in my dorm—the same cat he once watched, and it peed on his sheets. I digress. I live in the summer dorm, near the center of campus. He lives in the building right next to mine. I take summer school, an apprehensive writing class. He plays basketball, rehearsing for the highly anticipated season.

We see each other regularly, but our friendship lingers in the void. We have both become tied up with school obligations. My mild depression leads me to stay in my dorm most days. We make plans to see each other from time to time. I see him in passing almost daily as I leave for class, and he goes to the gym.

We have juvenile sex when it feels right, and text routinely.
Nothing and everything have changed.

Y.23

It's been over a month since summer school started.
Last night, he bid me to come and smoke pot in his car in the back of the library parking lot.

He sits in the driver's seat, toying with the music; I sit peacefully next to him. He is weary from the day. His once carefree smile is now burdened with the stress of expectations. The season will start in two months. It's all anyone talks about, him, how well he is going to play, and the team's potential. The bags under his eyes appear more cavernous than how I once remembered. He is physically changing, growing more muscular every day. I remain the same, tall, skinny, long light brown hair with red and blue extensions underneath, and my same green eyes. I wear gray baggy sweatpants, no bra under my white tank top. My face is makeup-free, and my hair hasn't been properly brushed in days. I wear cheap Victoria's Secret Love Spell body spray and large silver hoop earrings that brush against my aggressively bony shoulders.

I was already high when he eventually picked a spot to park. The tall LED lights from the parking lot informally illuminate his car. I pack the bowl, light the bowl, and inhale it tardily. He watches as the smoke laggardly lingers from my mouth and nose. I pass it to him, as he mirrors my actions. His hands almost double my size, making his blue and silver bowl seem unnaturally narrow. Our eyes soften as we both indulge.

Time passes, conversation ensues, and at some point, he had no choice but to journey to his dorm to retrieve something. What, I can't recall. I remained in his car.

He seldom considers others before himself. He is a naturally selfish individual. It isn't a defective character trait. He remains unapologetic. I can assume that this attribute contributes to his many achievements.

Gone no more than five minutes, when he reappeared, he had brought me a single packet of bright blue Welch's fruit snacks. I didn't ask for them, I didn't express the need for anything before he left, he brought them for me anyways. I smiled as we ate them together, continuing to smoke and talk.

This memory remains as one of the only times I ever sensed that he thought about me, too, perhaps even before himself.

Y.24

There is an intimacy that we share. We are misunderstood people, distinguishing who we want to be in the next chapter of our lives, how that would be orchestrated, and understanding that where we are is not our full potential.

Of our group of friends, it is evident that it will be the two of us who are going to do great things. It will be the two of us, who, unlike the others, are going to live a life worth writing about.

It is the two of us who have what it takes to make our dreams a reality.

Y.25

Midwest summer nights brew an allure that only those who have experience can characterize. The air heavy with potential. The conceivable optimism of driving with the windows down and allowing yourself to fondle the air. As the music grapples with you, you are irresistibly alive.

Driving in his car in the hours of darkness, withdrawing from our college town back to our city for the weekend. He divulged to me, jokingly proclaiming that he had the talent to tell the future. We sat parked in his mom's driveway. We, without fail, challenged each other. He always knew how to entice me, never fracturing eye contact. How can he tangibly tell my future? An impossible notion, but his adolescent wit remains persistent. We began to drive on the highway, the streetlights slightly illuminating the car. His face lit up, softly allowing his visage to become prevalently highlighted.

He revealed where he envisioned, we would both be in the coming year. I take a fancy to listening to him narrate what I was in store for. I adore the way his imagination worked. His references to SpongeBob make my heart giggle. I cherish how much of a kid he still is, mustering deliriously laughter with all the nonsensical shit he would convey to me. We played with each other. A comical back and forth, toying with one another.

We drove into the night, not a care in the world. Sinless conversation, untarnished by intruders. He was at his absolute self when he wasn't trying to impress anyone. When we are alone, I see the version of him I love.

Later that night we had sex, and it felt fucking good.

Y.26

He brings out the best in me.

Y.27

The summer between childhood and maturity overflowing with misfit adventures. We laugh perpetually that summer, we are the three best friends. Y, Ian, and I. Ian is the voice of reason, my protector. Y, he is always there to try to control my vagaries. I, the one always up to no good.

We smoked a lot of pot that summer, danced under the stars, drank when we could, and fucked each other like the children we were, and I fell in love with Y.

To put it quite simply, when I am with him, I am fervent.

Y.28

The summer is over.
    Today, we moved into our fall semester dorms.
    We are both in the same building, one floor apart.
    To put it lightly, I want to kill myself.
    I am grateful we are physically near each other.
    But loath this fact just as much.
    Things have mutated...

He came over today to help build our black futon which my roommate
bought from Target, and put his milk in our mini fridge.
    I don't know why he did that.
    His mom stopped by later to drop something off.
    Regrettably, I answered in just a towel.
    I sent him a picture of a kitten to make him smile.
    I hope it worked.
    I don't know how to navigate all the changes I can feel are coming,
    not just for me but for us.

We start college next week.

Y.29

At random, he gave me his bowl, which we use to smoke pot out of, to stash. We have smoked a lot of weed together with it. It is bonded to an incalculable amount of memories. It's no more than a few inches long, square, and decorated discreetly with lines of blue, silver, and gold. He gave it to me in a Clearasil box, used to conceal the smell. Conclusively, it has a name, all of us name them, but I can't revive the name at the given moment. He can't have it with him; he will be in deep water if anyone finds it. I don't know why, out of everyone, he bestowed it on me? I am unable to decipher if it is a fragile gesture of affection, a performance of appetency?

Regardless, I won't let anything happen to it.

We trust each other, and trust is harder to find than love.

Y.30

Happy Birthday, Relyuhcs.

imesssage, November 1ˢᵗ, 12:00 AM

Y.31

Last week, late Friday night, he enticed me to his dorm room.
I left the idiotic frat party I was at to clock in.
I laggardly lumbered into his dorm room,
He was having sex with another girl.
I shut the door immediately and bolted down the flight of stairs to my room.
I cried myself to sleep.
The whole floor audibly heard me sobbing hysterically.
Weepy from the abyss of my stomach, furiously.
I wish I didn't care about him.
I know he is sleeping with other girls. It doesn't bother me.
But seeing him do it –
His hands gripped the rope, suffocating me carnivorously.
Why did he call me to his room?
What did I ever do to deserve that?

The inauguration of my heart pulverized.
The first of many heartbreaks.

Y.32

He apologized.
  It took a week.
  I forgave him.
  That is what young girls are taught to do.

Y.33

He stopped by my dorm room to check on me today. A pattern he is committed to and repeats as often as he feels like. We wouldn't see each other or talk for a few days; I would start to savor the emancipation. Then, like clockwork, he would oblige me to remember him in whatever way he felt most compelled. He showed up unannounced, knocked on the cold, wooden door, and without hesitation let himself in. There was a demureness to the tribulation. He sat next to me on my neatly made dorm room bed, fiddling with my stuffed animals, our eyes both paralyzed, and we proceeded to make small talk.

"Are you okay?" He asked as his once familiar eyes inescapably cascaded vacantly over me. "Yeah, I am fine," I said, but all of me was lying.

I wanted to clamor out how I was losing my best friends, how miserable he unintentionally made me feel, how everything was changing so expeditiously, how I just wanted to be his favorite, how I would give anything just to go back three months ago when everything was perfect, how sitting across from him felt like a forced interaction we felt obligated to have just because we have sex, how nothing was the same, how, if we tried hard enough, we could make time stop just for a second and we could forget all the pandemonium.

Yeah, everything was fine.

A moment passed.

"I feel like I don't know you anymore," I said tepidly.
"You do. You know me better than anyone."

Y.34

If you want to know which girls are significant in his life, just look at his Twitter. I can find out everything I need to know. Both humiliating and gratifying to know I am one of them. He will make you feel novel by replying to you, favoring something you said, or retweeting you. Mostly, I find it childish and agitating. I have other infatuations in my life, but it never can go anywhere. He intimidates them. He is the most famous person at our school. Everyone follows him, whether on Twitter or Instagram. Everyone. He wants the entire university to know who is his so he can keep us all to himself. It's not rational.

Consequently, I hate all the other girls. I go to his page. I find them. I look at their pages. I admire their beauty and can agree that he has good taste. However, I deem them unintelligent with no evidence other than my jealousy. I get a rush of enraged irritation blazing from my heart. I close my phone. A few hours later, the process repeats.

Y.35

To know someone right before their dreams come true is to know someone at such a pivotal and powerfully violent time. I am witnessing him convert, I am watching him reconfigure. I watch on the sidelines as the friend I love so deeply becomes a stranger. Yet, I couldn't be prouder of him. At the expense of his ambitions coming true, our relationship began to delicately deteriorate.

Y.36

Five months into freshman year -

It didn't take me long to conceive that you need to assimilate your place in someone's life. You may perhaps suffer if you foresee too much. I assimilated this, the unmalleable way. I digested my place in his emergent life. Our teenage love was extinct. I developed into just another one of his many girls. I was the only foolish one who thought what we had when we were in high school made me the most important.

I have so much
Of you in my heart.

Y.37

Because I love you, I love her
   And her
   And her
   And her
   And her
   And her
   And her
   And her
   And her
   And her
   And her
   And her
   And her
   And her
   And her
   And her
   And her
   And her
   And her
   And her
   And her
   And her
   And her

And her
And her
And her
And her
And her
And her
And her
And her
And her
And her
And her
And her
And her
And her
And her
And her
And her
And her
And her
And her
And her
And her
And her
And her
And her
And her
And her
And her
And her
And her
And her
And her
And her
And her

Y.38

I hear your name exhaustively, everywhere I go.

    I can't escape you anywhere.

    You are on TV.

    You are on the billboards.

    You are all anyone wants to talk about.

    You are the number on everyone's jersey.

    I never mention your name.

    But you fucked me last night.

    You may be a god to everyone else, but to me, you're just average at best.

Y.39

Which brings me more pain?
   The misery of seeing you
   Or the misery of not seeing you?

Which brings me more torment?
   Fucking you
   Or knowing you're fucking her?

Which brings me more persecution?
   You telling the world about me
   Or you keeping me a secret?

Which brings me more ache?
   Loving you
   Or hating you ?

Y.40

He makes time for me, yes.
I assume passively that he hates when I sit courtside at his games and gawp
at him

Sometimes, I will smile at him; he will smile back.
Everything is discrepant now, you know?
Everything.

We aren't friends anymore.
We aren't a couple.
We fuck sometimes.
We talk often.
We see each other almost every day.

We bitterly tolerate each other, obligated by past teenage devotion.

Y.41

I will not think less of myself because you don't know how to be a good friend, a good person, or someone who knows how to love in any capacity. It must be horrifying to be inside your head. You have no regard for anyone else's feelings. Why should you? You were taught to be selfish, and it took control of you. I pity you.

You genuinely know only how to think about yourself.
   You must be so lonely.

Rest assured – he perceives me precisely the same way as I perceive him.
   We are one and the same.

Y.42

I grow more infuriated with his existence.

I always pretend not to know him. Not to see him. Taking the stairs to avoid him in the elevator. Denying his existence to anyone that brings him up. I live in a world where I no longer know him, the new him.

Y.43

It's the end of the school year.
  I was asked to an end-of-the-year frat formal by a boy.
  I said yes.
  Before heading to the party, a group of us decided to drink in the dorms.

I got ready for three hours. I took my time straightening my long brown hair. I wore a black tight dress that sparkled just right. I had black lace-up heels. My makeup was done, my nails were painted, and when I looked in the mirror, I felt desirable.

I animatedly walked to the end of the hallway, antsy to catch the elevator to head downstairs. My date and the party were expecting me. As the elevator opened, Y was there, standing alone.

His eyes diabolically met mine.
  Our relationship, as of late, was not composed of heartwarming affairs.
  Amounting to mostly late-night sex.
  Occasionally, seeing him out with another girl and pretending not to care.

"Where are you going?" He asked as I walked in.

I, without hesitation, turned my back towards him. I pressed deliberately hard on the button for the second floor. My eyes fixed on the closing metal doors.

"I have a date. I am going to a formal."

I could feel the heat of his annoyingly perfect body brushing up behind me. He grabbed my hips, turned me around, kissed me, and then pushed me gently away. As the elevator pinged carelessly, the doors began to slowly peel open; he looked me directly in the eyes.

"You are mine and you will always be mine. He knows, I know it, you know it."

After that night, everything changed.

Y.44

I want nothing to do with him and then sleep with him, so what does that say about me?

Y.45

Our relationship had amounted to nothing more than sleeping together and pretending to care about each other.

There would be bursts of happiness, but they never lasted long.

I stopped caring, and so did he.

It's a vague death.

When someone you know, when someone you care about, changes.

They become an unembellished stranger.

Word of advice,

They never come back, don't hold your breath.

Y.46

Despite everything, I still think I want him.
   Yes, I still want him badly.
   I get angry,
   I see him again.
   I get happy.
   His attention fuels me.

   I've been trying to discipline my heart not to want things it can't have.
It obeys, but my mind continues to defy what my humanity has long since
retained.

Y.47

He examined me.

He argued I was crazy.

And that's notably why he loved me.
And more notably, why he left.

Y.48

Laying on the cool, black, low to the ground table, I had no idea what the fuck I was doing. It only seemed right, getting a new tattoo in his apartment. I don't know the events that took place leading up to getting this tattoo. One second, a tattoo artist was coming to tattoo the team, the next, I was getting tattooed.

I am lying motionless on the table in his apartment. It is a high level of manic impulsivity. Tattooing nearly all of my right hip at twenty years old. I didn't think long or hard about getting the tattoo or what exactly I wanted. I decided the day before. The idea that it will permanently be on my body doesn't faze me.

He only saw me lying on the table for a moment. He walked in, stared at me, and went straight to his room. That's all I wanted, for him to know that even in his apartment, in front of his friends, I could do what I want.

The tattoo took hours.
The needles hit my skin.
I was mutating.
Physically and mentally.

This tattoo symbolizes a paradigm shift. The tattoo is my way of telling the world, myself, and him that the innocent girl is dead. Amongst witnesses, I slaughtered her.

Thus, the scorpion was born.

To this day, it remains my favorite and one of my most significant tattoos.

Y.49

We habitually had sex when high or drunk. Perhaps our age has something to do with it; we are both scared. Perhaps we are both embarrassed. Perhaps we need it as an excuse. Perhaps we have no idea what we are doing, but substances help us pretend. Perhaps if we have sex sober, it would certify our relationship. Perhaps it would create an incongruent relationship. It's rarely just us.

Y.50

I now strongly covet that our relationship never turned sexual because in doing so, it was the start of the end. Sex didn't bring us closer together; sex tore us apart. Excluding sex, I strongly believe we would still be in each other's lives to some gradation.

I don't think we fated to change as much or as hastily as we did. As the summer faded into our second year at university, it was the start of the end.

Y.51

Why can't I let you go?
   Why can't I let you go?
   Why can't I let you go?
   Why can't I let you go?
   Why can't I let you go?

Why can't I let you go?
   Why can't I let you go?
   Why can't I let you go?
   Why can't I let you go?
   Why can't I let you go?

Why can't I let you go?
   Why can't I let you go?
   Why can't I let you go?
   Why can't I let you go?
   Why can't I let you go?

Moving on has become an impaired enterprise, generous with resentment and self-torment. Everything in life has a purpose. I don't second-guess the role he played in my life. The circumstance of our relationship now only condones the distant memory of our time spent together.

Y.52

Did you ever care?
  Were you ever there?

What goes through your mind when someone says my name?
  Do you say anything? Or remain silent, making no claim.

At night, do you ever think of me?
  Fuck, marry, kill or all three.

It may have been months ago,
  But I would give the world to know.

Y.53

He slept with one of my friends, one of my best friends.
   At least, someone I thought was my friend.
   A year ago, he could never have done something like this to me.
   But now he can, and he did.
   The saddest part, I am not at all surprised.
   He doesn't owe me anything.

Y. 54

Do you stop caring for someone just because they betray you?
  You want to, but I think it's more complicated than that…

That's what makes the betrayal hurt, unusual:
  Anguish
  Resentment
  Wrath
  Malaise
  Grief
  Dejection

You feel it exhaustively, towards them, towards yourself.
  Logic and emotion contest.
  I sadly lost a friend.

Y.55

Two years later:

We both moved on with our lives.
We didn't speak.
We hardly saw each other.
It was assumedly the end.
Until I heard from him, once again.

Y.56

I was wearing a thigh-length, black silk skirt paired with a white lace halter top. My now blonde hair was half up, tied neatly back with a big bow, exposing all angles of my face. I had my nude strappy heels on and long, shoulder-length, silver sparkly earrings that shimmered delicately in the light. My friend was having a birthday party, and with nothing better to do, so I went.

It was a typical college pregame – music, beer, talking, standing around, gossiping, dancing, laughing. We were seniors now, reluctantly deciphering the last few months of being young. I didn't suspect anything of this night until he walked in.

We had been in the same place, seeing each other an infinite number of times in the past two years. We eventually harmonized, desensitized to each other, adapting to rapturously ignoring one another with ease. Tonight became the exception, commencing the bloodstained execution of our once unblemished adoration.

We instantaneously gravitated to each other. Our once magnetic attraction galvanized. Within twenty minutes, sitting alongside one another, talking as if no one else were in the room. That is entirely what was postulated. It was just him and me, two friends reconnecting, bedazzled over the last years of our lives. His unconstrained brown eyes, all over again, making acquaintances with mine. Time was immobile, as we laughed until tears assembled gaily in our eyes, just like when we were 17.

Our friends had to drag us out of the pregame, as we walked side by side to the bar that warm spring night. The conversation was flirtatiously ludic; we were back to innocently playing. We drank, we talked, we flirted – we were inseparable. Time rehabilitated whatever fallacious relationship we once endured.

I was aware of her. I knew he had a beautiful girlfriend for the last year or so. Knowing this, I left the bar by myself that night. I wanted to do the right thing. No sooner had I gotten home than my phone rang; it was him…

Y.57

The terror of loving someone matures as grimly as the dismay of someone loving me. I pray to overcome this. I am not sure how, but it will happen subsequently. I did it before, I can do it again.

Once more, when he called me early this morning to ask to use the extra bedroom in my apartment, I speculated annoyingly that he intends to move some of his belongings there. Regardless, I don't want to hear from him again. I deliberate painstakingly. It is in our best interest to stop talking to each other before it evolves into lethal mayhem that we both can't control. He makes neglecting him an impossible burden, communicating with me at all hours. I need to focus on myself and let stupid boys be predictable boys. I, horrendously, have a soft spot for him, which I hate, maybe because I used to revere him ineptly.

I am devoted powerlessly to the memories we made when nothing meant everything. Now, years later, everything means something, and it's quite draining.

Does his girlfriend really not know that he is sleeping with everyone, including her, including me? I had heard the rumors of him cheating on her for years. Now, confirming and contributing to those same rumors, now known facts.

I deprecate only myself. How can I be so frustrated when I catalyzed this behavior? Atrociously, I am as condemnable as he is. That's the thing about us: he is unquestionably the male version of me. We both can't help this unrestricted act of cruelty.

As much as I want to apologize for this affair, the part of me I hate is fucking addicted.

Y.58

We were happy for a month,
  but now I am mad.
  I have no right to be, but I am.

He isn't a man. He is a child.

He has no idea what it was like to take responsibility for anything in his life.
He treats females as disposable.

It must be such an endless hell to know that they only want to sleep with
him because he plays basketball. They don't want him, they just want his
potential, they want to tell their friends they slept with someone on the
team, not just someone, the best. They think they are special because he
will sleep with them.

It is pathetic to watch him get used to that extent.

It is such a desperate attempt to fill some sort of void he has buried inside
him. He is a sad excuse for a man, and the girls he is sleeping with behind
his girlfriend's back are pathetic. I am one of them. I am pathetic.

He has astonishingly low self-respect.

I don't want to be like them anymore.

I am not like them.

I am not going to allow him or anyone to treat me like this.

I am not going to allow him to treat his girlfriend like this.

He isn't anyone special, and just because he has fame, it doesn't mean he has power. He could control everyone but not me.

Y.59

I walked into the bar she worked at with ease.
I had no intention of unveiling our secrets that humid end-of-spring
afternoon.
I was demented, overflowing with wrathful distaste for the entire situation.
I didn't expect to see her there.
I wasn't aware she worked there.
I saw her and understood then what I had to do.
I walked up to her, stared at her, and blurted out,
"I am fucking your boyfriend."

Y.60

Despite once loving him, I can't lie for him, I can't lie to her about us. It will take every part of me to stand up for myself, to put myself and my feelings first. I watch the way he treated her, me, and the others. I don't want another person to have to experience such levels of disrespect. Last week, he has begged and begged for me to lie, to tell her I made it all up. To establish that I am some sort of crazy liar. I thought about it, I thought about risking my reputation to save his. Maybe years ago, I would have, but not anymore.

In these moments, I knew he changed me as well.

I will never lie for a man. Even though this ruined our friendship, the chances of me ever, to any degree, being in his life again.

I knew it was the right thing to do. I don't regret what I did. I never have, and I never will.

A weak woman will lie to protect the reputation of a man, a strong woman laughs even at the notion.

A lesson he had to learn the hard way.

Y.61

I was never going to get what I deserved from him.
I was never going to give him what he deserved from me.

Y.62

From time to time
  I think of then
  I twist my mind before again
  And though the memorandums are all a blur,
  I think of him
  And who we were.
  Invariably, on a whim
  I know you're happy with her.

From time to time
  I think of then
  I think of why, who, and when
  And where is he
  And what potential we could be
  I wonder if he thinks of me?

From time to time
  I think of then.
  Seeing you again
  2012 doesn't seem that far away
  How distant is yesterday
  The disastrous attempt at friends
  The catastrophe finally ends.

Y.63

I think, throughout the duration of our relationship, I mistakenly interpreted my feelings of friendship as feelings of love. I was never entirely in love with him, but not for lack of not trying. I was never in love with him because he never gave me the option. Perhaps I never really wanted it.

Y.64

He never forgave me for telling her, but more so, he never forgave me for not lying for him.

We went six years without speaking to each other, without seeing each other. I went six years existing as if he perished. The climax of our friendship, if you could call it that, was sinister, a dark, glowering evil. He gave me the confidence. Once I grasped my newfound power, he was repulsed by me. He had catalyzed the villain of his own story. I am not sorry for what I did, and I don't care if he has forgiven me or not; such is life.

The way that he cut me off was brutal. He cut off all access to him, out of pain or out of love, I'll never know. I found, from time to time, myself lost in contemplation of him. Lost, speculating where his NBA career was taking him, where he was, what he was doing, indispensably, if he ever thought of me, too. There was a warmth I felt when I reflected on him. I would occasionally try to search for any information about him, but the internet left me with a void. All the things I wanted to know about him, I couldn't find.

Six years later, we finally spoke again. Fate is funny, you know, and it just so happened we were in the same city at the same time.

He picked me up that sweltering summer afternoon. The sensation of seeing him was surreal. I was nervous, almost agitated, thinking about seeing him again. I wanted to be perfect, undamaged, unblemished, pristine. I never took the time to imagine what it might be like to see him again because I accepted that I would never see him again. In the six years, there were times when we were in the same place at the same time. I would leave before he even knew I was there. There were times when I knew he was going to be where I was, and I refused to go. I didn't want to see him; I thought seeing him would invoke disruptive suffering. I still had an ill-adjusted love for him. I accepted that I hurt him. I didn't want to face the consequences of my actions. That is how much I felt that he loathed me.

It was comparable to seeing an old friend. We didn't speak of the past, we caught up only on what we had both missed in each other's lives, but not in grave detail. It remained surface level. The exchange felt artificial. The answers I had longed for were not acquired. I regret not asking him more. When he had to leave, he didn't say goodbye to me.

That was the last time I saw him.
That was how our story ended.

Y.65

This heartbreak came from silence.
   From the goodbye we never said.
   From the last kiss that never happened.
   From the sorry never uttered.

The integral part
   of an inarticulate broken heart.

Y.66

During the time that I knew him, he was ambitious and aggressively determined. He chose what he wanted to become and became it. His life had purpose. He knew what he wanted out of life, and he was crazy enough not to stop until he had everything he had ever dreamed of. I saw the sacrifices he made, and I learned that from him. He showed me it was possible to have your wildest dreams come true. I wanted so badly to have access to his thoughts. I wanted to know how his brain worked, what it took to be someone who achieved their dreams. I admired him extremely. It was this admiration I had for him, this idolization of his ambition, that I was most attracted to.

I credit him because his drive and determination motivated me to write and continue to write to this day. He gave me conviction. He taught me to never settle for anything less than my dreams coming true. He was the first person to make me feel beautiful. He was the first person to teach me that I had worth.

To say I loved him would discredit what he meant to me. He was my true friend. I cared for him immensely, so. I still do. He is without a doubt the hardest worker I have ever met. His dedication to his art is admirable to everyone around him.

His heart and my heart are very old friends.
He was a dream, then a reality, now just a fond memory.

How to Turn a Boy Into a Man

Part one:

Make a boy suffer the consequences of his actions. Never feel guilty about doing the right thing, even if it hurts, even if you love that boy, even if you lose that boy. A boy will need to be shared and surrounded by not only you, but many other beautiful women, a man does not. Don't tolerate this. The lonely boy is just looking for love in all the wrong places, hold sympathy for the insecure. Lastly, never lie to protect a boy's reputation.

These lessons, coupled with others found later in this book, will aid in teaching a boy to be a man.

N

20 years old

Intertwined directly with time.
& the lessons cultivated by the clock.
Sorrowfully vying with the heart,
When to hold on & when to let go.

N.1

Sitting on the oyster grey, decrepit sectional watching TV, there he was. I have seen him before around campus. I don't know anything about him. Freshly friends with his roommate, I was welcomed into his apartment that blistering late August afternoon.

I don't recollect much of what we talked about. I wasn't listening to him. I was there, participating in the conversation, but mostly I was enclosed by my dialogue. Say all the right things, things to impress him, things to warrant continuous conversation. Keep him engrossed.

I undoubtedly met a boy who stimulated me.
Little did I know then that years of stimulation amounting to excruciating mental convulsions were to transpire.

N.2

It's been two weeks since we were first introduced. It took only a few days for us to become fast friends.

It's an enigmatic, sort of, lightning connection I feel toward him. I think we knew each other from a past life.

He walked over to my apartment to hang out earlier today. I answered the door to his tall, dark, muscular body towering over me as he leaned in to give me a hug. My small, teenage girl-like figure fits perfectly encapsulated in him. His full lips, outlined by a coarse beard, complement the roundness of his full face. We sat across one another, my kitchen table separating us, as we talked about nothing the whole night. He caught me smiling at him. He smiled back.

N.3

I am awake, it's early for me
    Should I text him, "Good morning, I can't sleep"?
    I shouldn't
    But…

"Good morning,
I can't sleep."

I lay awake, amiably with a smile on my face, lusting for his reply.

N.4

He is back home, and I am here finishing my third year of summer school. I miss him. I miss being with him. Inevitably, we talk morning, noon, and night. I ask him for guidance on a fair amount of things - what picture I should post on Instagram, at school, and everything in between. Our trust grows systematically.

The phone rang last night; I wasn't expecting anyone, and a smile appeared on my face when I saw it was him on FaceTime. He was ever so innocently cooking fresh and juicy lobster in his mother's kitchen. The whole thing was hilarious, his creole accent so savory to my ears, flushed with his garrulous mumbling – ah, I am in love with his voice.

We intoxicate each other with mirthful laughter. The entity of our conversation was so powerful that time became irrelevant. I laid in bed as we talked hours under the mysteries of the summer moonlight and early into the flaming morning.

He already knows me prodigiously well, comfortably apprehensive of me. I am waiting eagerly for him to come back to town.

N.5

I walk over to his apartment regularly, a close twenty-minute walk from mine. We spend time together. It is unadulterated contentment. Being in each other's presence is sufficient for both of us. He helps me with my day-to-day endeavors. He gives me relationship advice for the boys I have a crush on and getting over Y is not easy. We go out to our local college bar, grab drinks and food, talk for hours, laugh about nothing, and watch cartoons. When we aren't together, we are incessantly communicating. He tells me of his life back home and his family, and he tells me about his little brothers and his adoration for them. He acquainted me with his friend group; his friends are becoming my friends. Our lives are blissfully intertwined.

N.6

His heart is immense, bursting with boundless love, exploding onto those around him. I celebrate it. He could never hurt a fly. He provides extraordinary quantities of love to those around him. The way he values his companionships is admirable; he is willing to go to war for any of them. His loyalty to those he loves is steadfast in the face of any temptation. I can see so clearly that he gives more love than he receives. That's just in his nature. He's a strong yet highly sensitive individual. A severed angel. He puts other people's needs before his own, often forgetting to take care of himself. I think over time, the love he so unselfishly gives out without any return will damage him irreversibly. I have never met someone like him. N is something special; everyone seems aware of this, except him. He isn't an accident. The world begs persistently for more people like him.

N.7

It's growing arduous, attempting to translate my sensibilities.
   I love him very dearly as my best friend.
   Now and again, I find myself loving him in an anthologized way.
   The way, you know, where you burn to see them naked.

N.8

I thirst for nothing from him except for his time. For virtually six months, I have slept alongside him every night, retiring in his arms, and coming to life every morning next to him. One of the earliest occasions I wrote about him was a single line, "He is my sunshine." I feel secure with him; I feel like he is protecting me. No one can hurt me when I am with him. I am becoming enamored with this sentiment. We do everything together. We are simply inseparable. I am falling in love with him, and concurrently, I am pleading with my heart. I understand I can't have him. I am keeping my fixation for him close to me. I have revealed to no one that I am falling in love with him.

N.9

I am getting ready for bed in his room. It's a small, perfectly square, one-bedroom oasis. The room is simple – a bed, a dresser, a TV. He gives me one of his Nike T-shirts to sleep in, the same one from the night before. I have slept over almost every night this week. I make him leave the room as I undress. He has never seen those parts of my body. I yell for him to come in once I am finished changing. He smiles when he opens his bedroom door. We crawl into bed together, slipping under his red cotton sheets. I sleep on the left, he on the right. His body is almost double the size of mine. All 6'2 of him wraps himself around me, hugging me tightly. I fit perfectly underneath his arm.

"What do you want to watch?" He said, still squeezing my body into his.
"Family Guy."

He brushes my hair away from my face, squeezes me tightly, and kisses my forehead. We both fall asleep in each other's arms.

N.10

Be Mine. Be Mine. Be Mine. Be Mine. Be Mine. Be Mine. Be Mine. Be Mine. Mine. Be

Mine. Be Mine. Be Mine. Be Mine. Be Mine. Be Mine. Be Mine. Be Mine.
Be Mine. Be Mine. Be Mine. Be Mine. Be Mine. Be Mine. Be Mine. Be
Mine. Be Mine. Be Mine. Be Mine. Be Mine. Be Mine. Be Mine. Be Mine.
Be Mine. Be Mine. Be Mine. Be Mine. Be Mine. Be Mine. Be Mine. Be
Mine. Be Mine. Be Mine. Be Mine. Be Mine. Be Mine. Be Mine. Be Mine.
Be Mine. Be Mine. Be Mine. Be Mine. Be Mine. Be Mine. Be Mine. Be
Mine. Be Mine. Be Mine. Be Mine. Be Mine. Be Mine. Be Mine. Be Mine.
Be Mine. Be Mine. Be Mine. Be Mine. Be Mine. Be Mine. Be Mine. Be
Mine. Be Mine. Be Mine. Be Mine. Be Mine. Be Mine. Be Mine. Be Mine.
Be Mine. Be Mine. Be Mine. Be Mine. Be Mine. Be Mine. Be Mine. Be
Mine. Be Mine. Be Mine. Be Mine. Be Mine. Be Mine. Be Mine. Be Mine.
Be Mine. Be Mine. Be Mine. Be Mine. Be Mine. Be Mine. Be Mine. Be
Mine. Be Mine. Be Mine. Be Mine. Be Mine. Be Mine. Be Mine. Be Mine.
Be Mine. Be Mine. Be Mine. Be Mine. Be Mine. Be Mine. Be Mine. Be
Mine. Be Mine. Be Mine. Be Mine. Be Mine. Be Mine. Be Mine. Be Mine.
Be Mine. Be Mine. Be Mine. Be Mine. Be Mine. Be Mine. Be Mine. Be
Mine. Be Mine. Be Mine. Be Mine. Be Mine. Be Mine. Be Mine. Be Mine.
Be Mine. Be Mine. Be Mine. Be Mine. Be Mine. Be Mine. Be Mine. Be
Mine. Be Mine. Be Mine. Be Mine. Be Mine. Be Mine. Be Mine. Be Mine.
Be Mine. Be Mine. Be Mine. Be Mine. Be Mine. Be Mine. Be Mine. Be
Mine. Be Mine. Be Mine. Be Mine. Be Mine. Be Mine. Be Mine. Be Mine.
Be Mine. Be Mine. Be Mine. Be Mine. Be Mine. Be Mine. Be Mine. Be
Mine. Be Mine. Be Mine. Be Mine. Be Mine. Be Mine. Be Mine. Be Mine.
Be Mine. Be Mine. Be Mine. Be Mine. Be Mine. Be Mine. Be Mine. Be
Mine. Be Mine. Be Mine. Be Mine. Be Mine. Be Mine. Be Mine. Be Mine.
Be Mine. Be Mine. Be Mine. Be Mine. Be Mine. Be Mine. Be Mine. Be
Mine. Be Mine. Be Mine. Be Mine. Be Mine. Be Mine. Be Mine. Be Mine.
Be Mine. Be Mine. Be Mine. Be Mine. Be Mine. Be Mine. Be Mine. Be
Mine. Be Mine. Be Mine. Be Mine. Be Mine. Be Mine. Be Mine. Be
Mine. Be Mine. Be Mine. Be Mine. Be Mine. Be Mine. Be Mine. Be Mine.
Be Mine. Be Mine. Be Mine. Be Mine. Be Mine. Be Mine. Be
Mine. Be Mine. Be Mine. Be Mine. Be Mine. Be Mine. Be Mine...

N.11

We bankrupt the day together. I love him. He loves me. That's all.

N.12

I fantasize about you.
   About being alone with you
   About all the things I would do for you

N.13

His heart is too valuable just to give away.
  I must garner it.
  He is grueling to love.
  I don't want to steal his heart.
  I want him to feel safe enough to give it to me.
  He has been hurt badly before.
  This will take time.
  I am patient.

N.14

I think I've always had a thing for defective people.

I think I have always had a thing for damaged people.

I feel the need to help them.

I feel the need to understand them.

I feel the need to be a part of their lives, no matter the consequences.

I want to fix them because I can't fix myself.

But N, he is trying to fix me.

Our group of friends all went together to a house party last night. I don't remember much of the night. I woke up to him addressing me mercilessly, upset with the amount of alcohol I consumed. He reeled off my deeds. I question if he was telling me the truth. He said I embarrassed myself, taking too many shots, kissing a random boy, and throwing up once I got back to his apartment. What does he expect? I am barely 21 years old. I can do what I want; I don't need another parent.

N.15

We had sex last night, after all this time.

    Fuck. Shit. Damn it.

    This was not in the plan.

    We were supposed to be best friends and only that.

                    Everything has been abruptly destroyed.

N.16

I am your secret.
  But you are my oath.

No one knows we have been sleeping together. No one knows that our relationship has mutated from friends to something more. Having sex has changed our dynamic, pushing our relationship into a new paradigm. It is not better or worse, but it is different. I am adjusting.

N.17

The world is a cruel place full of misery, suffering and despair. It is his brilliance that keeps me suspended. I look forward every day to talking to him, seeing him, and touching him. Being in his presence alone is an endowment. With him it is the minuscule moments that actualized the love we share.

The way that he loves is distinctive, in a curious and timorous way. He is navigating how to love me, as I am doing the same. It is youthful, it is halcyon.

N.18

Our most profound bonding happened while our relationship was a secret. The first time we had sex, the first time I told him I loved him, sleeping next to him night after night, drinking late nights in his apartment, elaborately expending all our free time together… creating such fond memories. We maintain a confidential relationship even now.

In the back of my head, I know that this isn't tangible. It's a secluded, polygamous, twisted vow to one another. I can't talk to my friends about it. We don't talk about it.

I am incarcerated by my thoughts, analyzing unfathomably how we got to this perplexing saga of vexatious oblivion.

N.19

Being together but not actually being together pulverizes everything.

This "relationship" was doomed the moment I opened my legs.
Falling victim to the curse of a stealth affair.
Both so frustrated and annoyed with one another that we ended things.

Going from best friends to blocked.
From sleeping together to not being able to make eye contact.
It's agonizing how human interaction can be reconstructed so
expeditiously.

From lovers to strangers in mere moments.

N.20

Everything is gone
  I hope you're happy
  My soul is moving on

N.21

The following is a collection of writings that span across
three years –

Tormented excessively, stalled at the extremities of releasing & remaining.

N.22

One day, he began talking to her again.

After a year of silence, there it was, his voice. I treasure his almost somber baritone articulation. His modulated, thick voice composes serenity in me, reviving a repressed stillness. It has such profound power over me.

His voice gave her exiguous hope that one day, soon, she would see him again.

N.23

Late, he lies awake in bed.
  Delving into the cosmos inside his head
  Universes start to flourish in his sleep
  And he dances closely in the sinister and deep
  Colliding with the boat of dreams
  He sails through the lavender seams
  All the cares and doubts of his day
  Dissolve and drift away

N.24

It's your voice that undresses me
  The potential your articulation embodies
  Enunciation that dominates my consciousness
  Every time you speak
  I lose my heart to you

N.25

Fatal attraction,
 That's the best way to describe what we have.
 An intense and obsessive morbid infatuation with one another.
 My thinking lacks reason and logic.
 This causes me to have a negative impact on him.
 It's unhealthy and dangerous, a physiological need –

                                        Substance abuse.

N.26

It's been months since we reconnected.

   I miss the relationship we once had.

I am holding on to the hope that what we have now will somehow morph into what we had before. I am tortured. I love you and I care about you in an unrestrained manner. I have immeasurable resentment for how much I overindulge. I am petrified that sooner or later, you will cultivate resentment toward me. Abandoning me once more, and I can't endure it. I can't lose you again. We end things, we get back together, we end things, we get back together. I love you achingly, blisteringly… I fucking hate it. Experiencing every single day, striving to please you, preserving this derangement. But I don't know how to be without you. I am depressed. You don't care about me the same way, it's undeniable. Why can't I let you go?

N.27

It's exhausting loving you more than you love me
   I think about us
   And you think about her
   I think about what can be
   And you think about being free
   And to some fucked up degree
   Even after I pleaded
   You disagree
   With you, goodbye is always guaranteed.

N.28

We are not together yet…

I feel obligated to him
   I must be loyal to him
   In my head, he is mine
   In my head, our relationship appears intrinsic

I am lying on the dark red floor of excruciating eternal hell.

N.29

I am always there waiting for him when he comes back.
  It is sad and pathetic, but I love him, so I don't care.

N.30

Once again, I am his and he is mine. We still aren't a couple. We still aren't anything more than friends. I long for more than he can provide me. The first two years of our relationship were spent with secrets. I know he has others, and so do I.

Fundamentally, I speculated his affection for me was heavier than mine; it hasn't taken long for the emotions I had for him to exceed anything I reached before. I am petrified to tell him anything. I am uneasy about how it might transfigure our new "friendship". I have never figured out how to show sentiment properly. I can't comprehend what I am feeling and why I am feeling it. These last two years, I have lived in agony trying to impress him, show him I am enough, and make him love me. It is self-destruction. I have collapsed. Now, I start to destroy him. I will go to extraordinary lengths to try to heal us. I spend many nights crying in sorrow over our relationship. I spend many nights going to bed with a smile because of him. I don't know what to do.

N.31

I hate that he doesn't accommodate me. I hate that he doesn't pursue me. I hate that he can so effortlessly block me from contacting him. I hate that I am his sin. I hate the other girls he fucks. I hate that he doesn't put me first. I hate weeping over him. I hate how desperate and dire I am for his attention. I hate that his attention feels essential to my survival. I hate how pathetic he makes me feel. I hate the capacity he has over my emotions. I hate that he feels ashamed of me. I hate writing about him. I hate the sheer evil he provokes in me. I hate what our relationship has come to. I hate him because loving him is harder.

I love that he accommodates me. I love that he pursues me. I love that he can so effortlessly unblock me to contact him. I love that I am his sin. I love the other girls he fucks. I love that he puts me first. I love weeping with joy over him. I love how desperate and dire I am for his attention. I love that his attention feels essential to my survival. I love how unpathetic he makes me feel. I love the capacity he has over my emotions. I love that he doesn't feel ashamed of me. I love writing about him. I love the sheer love he provokes in me. I love what our relationship has come to. I love him because hating him is harder.

N.32

Things between us have gotten so bad.
  I don't know what to do anymore.
  I did everything I could.

What do you say when you're not enough to make someone stay?
  When you're not enough for them?

N.33

I am excessively possessive of him. He is the one that I don't want to share.
I know how he loves a person, and once you experience that rendition of
love, you want it all to yourself.

> *His love has become imperative to my existence.*
> *His love is deranging me from logic.*

We are poisonous towards each other, both drinking from the same cup. We
have actualized a sinuous version of our emblematic hell, which neither of
us can escape. I can not be with him. I can not be without him. Toxic does
not scratch the surface of how destructive our relationship has amounted
to. The more I feel I need him, the more he pushes me away.

I saw him last night at the bar with two girls.
  A rage escalated inside me.
  I had lost the capability to control myself.
  I couldn't bear the thought of another girl having him.
  I began to scream at them, becoming this maniacal version of myself.
  He was taunting me, aware of the feelings it would exacerbate.
  It took my entire being to restrain myself from physically assaulting them,
  As I hissed every verbal insult I could contrive.
  Lashing out at two complete strangers who did not do one thing wrong.
  I had gone, in all respects, psychotic.

I left, as he sneered at me, and effectively, I had been defeated.

Later that night, I was naked in his bed.
   And that's how we loved each other.
   These are the games we played.

N.34

He texted me to tell me he missed me and loved me today.
I get so close to moving on, and then he comes back.
We love each other, and for every bad thing I write, I can write ten good things.
Why do we love each other like this?
Why can't we be conventional?

What we have continues to industrialize into a malicious entity fostering nefarious love.

N.35

We are sorry
   The number you're trying to reach
   Blocked you a long time ago
   Hang up and never call again.

N.36

It's done.
We can no longer stand each other in any way, shape, or form.

I argue that I will still love him. Getting over him is an impossible task. I have accepted that maybe it will never happen, that I will spend my whole life missing him, loving him, wanting to be with him. I spent hours, days, and months trying to forget him. It feels unachievable and implausible.

I don't want him to be a lesson learned the hard way.
I was left worse by my wanting.

N.37

I
Am
Lonely
Without
Him

Missing someone who doesn't miss you back is mental humiliation.
I wonder how many years it will take to erase you from me?

I wash you off me.
I want to be free.

N.38

Two years later…

He emerged in my inbox—a simple message, saying hi. I was lying in my bed, scrolling into oblivion, when it came through. I didn't expect it. The last two years have been blissful without him in my life. I still thought about him from time to time, but I had reasoned that he would never return. Although it took time, I had made peace with that fact. At first, I thought I was seeing things. Our last conversation consisted of me texting him the foulest of things, digging into him with words for daggers in hopes of destroying any potential of us getting back together. I felt that this was the only way to stop the cycle, doing and saying things so unforgivable that he would never want to come back into my life. Yet, here we are. We have started to talk as friends again, for a month or so.

I have the conviction that we will be able to make a friendship work.
I still love him so much.
I will do anything for one more chance.

N.39

Inconsequentially, we both tried, yet we would always, without rationale, end up back in each other's lives. I want this pattern to have a purpose. I believe, to my depths, that he is destined to be in my life permanently. That the reason we can't be without each other is, because we are, in fact, meant to be.

It didn't work last time, or the time before that, but this time is different.

It is profound, serpentine insanity.

N.40

Three months ago, we finally decided to see each other in person.

  We have to make it work. This time is different.

I am taking this as a frivolous declaration of our love for one another. We live too far away to drive to see each other, the distance requires a flight, and a flight requires money. We have both been taking turns flying to see one another as often as we can. We both work, so finding time has been difficult. We both aren't making great money. It is becoming a financial burden, which is making things debilitating. We both have less-than-ideal living situations, which also makes seeing each other grueling.

It doesn't matter, we are making it work, despite every curveball we are being thrown.

This time is different.

N.41

What's more fearsome?
   Telling someone you're in love with them?
   Or telling someone you're still in love with them?

N.42

I love him. I am in love with him. Our relationship is perfect. It's been an amazing last three months. Then something happens. We get into a fight. The fight to end all fights. I fucking hate him. I wish I had never met him. We break up; it's not going to work. We take a few weeks apart to both realize what we really wanted, and now we've decided to get back together.

I love him. I am in love with him. Our relationship is perfect. It's been an amazing last three months. Then something happens. We get into a fight. The fight to end all fights. I fucking hate him. I wish I had never met him. We break up, it's not going to work. We take a few weeks apart to both realize what we really wanted, and now we've decided to get back together.

Repeat.
Repeat.
Repeat.

This is our relationship.
We have plummeted into the same sequence of torture.

N.43

Logic and reason take no part in our turbulent relationship. Loving him is a rare privilege that few in this world will experience. Matched by an equally throbbing death. Under no circumstances do I want to love him the way I do; it just sort of happened, gradually at first, and without warning, it has taken hold of me entirely.

We both have such a jarred way of articulating love. Once we started damaging each other, we never stopped. It is a disturbed war where we hate each other yet love each other with the same amount of vigor.

We are both intent on destroying the other one.

N.44

It is safer for me to suffer before him naked
    than to enunciate my inclinations
    Inducing warfare,
    Becoming an impenetrable siege

It is safer for me to implement a ceasefire
    to lie on my back and
    Unlock my legs,
    Becoming fatally silent

It is safer for me to utter
    "Make love to me."
    Withholding the crusade,
    Becoming an unpronounced casualty

It is dangerous to say
    "Love me and only me."
    Extracting carnage
    Becoming complacent in combat

The blood of validity stained by desire.

N.45

I hurt him because I cared. I was too inexperienced to perceive anything different. He hurt me to shield his heart. He had to protect me, but he had to protect his heart first. That was something I could never understand.

N.46

He invited me to Kansas City for the weekend to celebrate the birthday of one of his best friends. I was thrilled, euphoric even—it was another opportunity to spend the weekend together. I envisioned perfection, lovers' exultation.

I was drastically incorrect.
It was one of the worst weekends of my life.
He humiliated me.

Most of the weekend, I spent alone in the hotel room we were sharing. He was getting drunk and high with his friends. What little time we were together, he ignored me. I don't know why I was even there.

Saturday night, the group of us went to the club for his friend's birthday. I left early. I begged him to leave with me so we could spend time together before I had to get on my flight home the next day. I was trying to salvage what little time we had left together. He wanted to stay out.

He never came back to the hotel room.

I want to remember exactly how I felt lying on the floor of that hotel, crying my eyes out, realizing I wasn't in love with him.

I never want to forget.

In the morning, I woke up, and he still wasn't there next to me. He stayed out all night, doing God knows what.

He left me to asphyxiate on my angst. I left, got on my flight, and vowed to myself never to speak or see him again.

I committed.

It was over.

I cried the entire flight home.

That was the end.

N.47

When we said goodbye, I went through all my old writings, frantically, searching for him on every page, searching for the first time I wrote about him. Digging relentlessly so I could remember how he made me feel. What words you brought out of me. How beautiful we had been.

When I found it, the first time I wrote about you, the first time we had sex, the first fight, the lasting heartache I felt over the last year. When I reread everything, I was reminded of what I already knew. We could not make it work. How badly I wanted you. Everything I read was just a reminder of how much time, energy, and how much of myself I had given to this relationship. It was failing, and I felt like I was failing by giving up. My mind knew long before my heart. Yet, I can't let you go. Why can't I let you go?

N.48

Accept those things that end.
   I can't accept that this is the end.
   How can it be the end?
   The end means forever, the end means forever.
   I don't want to give up.
   Giving up means saying goodbye
   I can't imagine my life without him.
   Yes, it was debilitated from the start.
   I never had the chance to love him the way I wanted to.

We never chose to have a conventional relationship, and this was six years
of diabolical love.

N.49

I am trying relentlessly to unlearn him. I want to erase him, and any memory, person, or place associated with him. I collapsed. He has never left my mind. I am aggravated every day with thoughts of him.

I am trying to move on.
I know I can continue without him.

N.50

You can let go.
    I am finally okay on my own.
    I am over you.
    I made it through.

N.51

You will always have the memories.
   That is what he became to me, just a memory.

One Year Later…

N.52

I know we are both crazy, but I am happier with him than without him.

N.53

Throughout the last year and a half of our relationship, after seeing each other a handful of times, we have decided again that it isn't going to work. He isn't the love of my life. We are too broken to love each other in a healthy way. Even after knowing this, we still haven't stopped seeing each other. I am living in Chicago. He has come to the city to visit his family. These trips have ended up shedding light on what we had previously tried to conceal. He always stops by and sees me. We never spent more than a few hours together. We smoke, fuck, and say goodbye. I realize that this is the healthiest we have ever been, because I expected nothing from him.

N.54

I accepted that we were not meant to be together. After years of fighting what I knew to the great depths, touching me fundamentally, I surrendered irrevocably to those feelings. That winter day in Boston, I sat across from him, and I started to cry. Once I started to cry, I couldn't stop. These tears weren't hyperactive; they were slow and poetic. I poured over the person I had loved so deeply, so passionately, so vehemently, and forfeited all my sentiments.

For years, I had tried to change him. For years, I overlooked characteristics that I knew I didn't want in a partner. For years, we had tried to force something that was never going to transpire which resulted in such hatred for each other. For years, I couldn't love him, I only loved the person that I pined for him to be.

As I sat across from him, tears dripping from my eyes, I felt gargantuan relief for the first time. It wasn't that I gave up on him or gave up on the love that we shared. I irrevocably comprehended that he was not the love of my life, no matter how much I wanted him to be. I didn't want to try to change him anymore, he was fucking perfect. He was just not perfect for me. At that moment, I finally saw how beautiful he was.

I knew I was never going to see him again. I knew it was over. It was completed. I think he sensed it, too.

It remains the greatest phenomenon of my life, for at that moment, I knew that after all these years, I was finally free.

N.55

Every time we would get back together, I would expect it to be different, but it never was. We repeated the same cycle unremittingly until we both wore each other out. We loved as if we had all the time in the world. I never wanted to give up on him. He never wanted to give up on me. We afforded our relationship more time than we should have. He is incredibly special to me because everything I learned about love, life, pain, and heartbreak synchronously, we learned the same things. Over the six or so years, he taught me an extraordinary amount about life, how to love, and most importantly, how to let go.

How To Turn A Boy Into a Man

Part Two:

One of the most torturous and exhausting lessons in life can be learning the art of detachment. You can teach a boy to be a man by letting go. Time and trauma can create what feels like an unbreakable bond between two people. Time spent doesn't equate love. Don't be fooled. To teach a boy to be a man, you must gather the strength to say goodbye and never look back.

These lessons, coupled with others found later in this book, will aid in teaching a boy to be a man.

X

24 years old

He has had an incredible impact on the trajectory of my life.
The first boy to expose me as a writer.
& with staggering vengeance, we annexed a pernicious affair.

Death, sex, writing, and the pursuit of happiness.

X.1

When we met, I knew exactly who he was. I look back now and often contemplate what he saw in me. Why that day? Why did he come up to me? What were his intentions? The fortitude of that conversation was something I had most certainly extracted as unprecedented, almost vehement.

"Hi, it's nice to meet you. I saw you walk in, and I wanted to come say hello. Allow me to introduce myself…"

X.2

Three days later -
  02:00

"Come to the window."
  He was there.
  "Come downstairs."
  I went.
  "Come with me."
  I followed.

We walked hours into the velvet twilight of the night sky, sauntering through the wonderful silence of our sleeping city. The illumination from the orb of the silver moon cast light down upon us. Intensified by the perspiring air, my mouth sipped the taste of impassive quietude. Time melted like the forgotten carton of ice cream left out on the kitchen counter. As golden cotyledons began to eat away the forgiving darkness, with ease we confessed both our dreams and sins.

Bound within us was a congruent evil – we trusted each other.

X.3

Last night, I had a dream about him.
  I wonder if he dreamt about me, too.

It felt so real.

Where instead of reality, I was his.

And life was exquisitely cheerful.
  And we were hypnotized with one another.

X.4

We sit across one another. I delve into his eyes, investigating them laboriously. I can't read him. I am baffled by the vacuous, left wondering who broke his heart. Who was before me? How did they eradicate his delicate paradoxes? I am left with half a man. I require more. The smell of his flesh ventilates as he sings his secrets. I watch, I listen. His eyes remain perished. I speculate as he sermonizes - is everything that comes out of his mouth a lie? Unfrightened by my accusation, I only want him more.

X.5

A letter he wrote to me, placed on the side of our bed.
  We have known each other for eighteen days.

"I need you
I fucking need you
I have to have you

Can't you see
You've made a monster out of me?"

X.6

We've spent the last two days in the recording studio.
   We've spent the last two days creating,
   We've spent the last two days writing,

He is so talented.
   He is so smart.
   He is so determined.

My words have never had such meaning.
   My desire to become a writer is as rigorous as it has ever been.
   My stories are being brought to life like never before.

When we are together, I write about him.
   When we are apart, I write about him.
   When I have the pen in my hand, I write about him.

X.7

I wake up in our bedroom. The morning sun beautifully glides across the white silk bed sheets. The window is cracked, open freely, allowing the warm air to leisurely join me, imbuing the room. The sheer floor-length curtains pirouette across the wood floor. The air is restorative. I didn't feel him next to me. It wasn't unusual for me to wake up unaccompanied. He customarily wakes up before me, leaving me to dream as long as I please.

While I sleep, he departs, fetching breakfast, a bouquet of fresh red roses, and the day's fashion magazines. Patiently, he lingers, waiting for me to wake up, filling his morning by scribbling song melodies outside on the small rustic balcony that overlooks the sedulous city below.

I wander to the kitchen while gently rubbing my eyes, fondling the first minutes of the morning. My hair pulled back into a messy bun with small pieces of my hair scattered, framing my oval face. I wear nothing. My feet glide, dancing across the floor as I make my way to him.

We fuck every morning on the kitchen counter, sometimes the balcony for the world to see. He serves me breakfast at the table. It's how we start our day. I remain naked as he asks me about my dreams. Smiling, he praises my writing from the day before. He haphazardly sips his coffee as he asks me what I will write about today.

We start the day.

X.8

It's been nearly a month since we first met. I know it seems quick, but I am going to let him read it—all of it. I finally am. I am going to allow someone access to the most sacred part of myself, my journal.

I am naked.
   It feels dangerous.

Has anything ever felt wrong?
   You know it's wrong.
   But you do it anyway.

You do it anyway because you would hate yourself for not doing it.

I AM GOING TO DO IT.

I think I am going to do it.

I did it.
My secrets have been shattered.

X.9

I find myself reading back over my writings about him in these early hours of the morning, and it's either a work of art created by an insane genius or ineffectual sediment created by a wannabe writer.

Everything I write is for him or about him.
   He never leaves my mind.
   I am becoming enthralled with what he brings out of me.
   He is making me a writer.
   I am making him my muse.

I am devoted to the art we synthesize.

X.10

Our relationship is electrifying. He is the first person I have shared my quintessence so vulnerably with. It has granted me a fresh, bountiful way to attach to someone. We work collectively to construct eloquent songs, poems, and oeuvres. We are one and the same; we want the same things. It translates effortlessly from the pen to the bedroom.

X.11

Love is easy. I love so many people. However, trust? Trust is rare. I trust him. He creates a safe environment for my primitive expression. The reason I started to write my first novel is because of him. He pushes me. He encourages me. He won't let me not write. We hold nothing back. The honesty is refreshing. It is elementary, barring no complications. He brings out things and words in me that I had not known possible. Unlike the others, he isn't afraid of his emotions or mine. He embraces his feelings. He teaches me to do the same. He teaches me not to fear what I am feeling or why I am feeling it, but to harness it and use it to create. It is working.

X.12

After I let him read my journals, staring at me dreadfully, he whispered, "You write so openly. Your innermost thoughts are horrifying. Thank you."

X.13

You always divulged,
    The female body is the clearest triumph,
    The divine feminine.

You sculpted your masterpiece.
    You illustrated me
    You sanctioned my essence
    You assigned me intention
    You clenched my body and erected art
    I am enamored with the aptitude of your dexterity

X.14

"Let's go away this weekend," he said, dressing for the day ahead. He takes his time with everything he wears, down to the smallest detail. Incredibly aware of how to dress, I find his style irresistible. "I'll take you anywhere you like." I don't reply right away. I marinate with the proposal. I sit naked, cross-legged on the floor of the closet. I hardly see the need to dress anymore, we fuck every hour or so. I simply learned it was a waste of time to bother reclothing myself. He stands over me, scrolling through his leather jackets, humming to himself. "So, where do you want to go?" He says again as if I didn't hear him the first time, now focusing his attention on me.

"Take me to your house. Where do you live?" I challenged him, knowing damn well he would never dare allow me access. I have no idea where he lives; we only ever stay in homes he has rented temporarily, hotels, and Airbnbs. I imagine he must have a house somewhere. If he were to be so bold as to take me there, I could get answers to long overdue questions.

"Anywhere but there." He hissed, now standing directly over me. He smirked devilishly and continued browsing the jackets. He could do that, be so happy one moment, and in the next be filled with anger. There was no point in replying.

X.15

Our relationship is a collaborative affair. Feeding and living off one another. We are dedicated to performing important roles in the ecosystem that exists inside one another. He is the dominant species, allowing our relationship to be competitive and diverse. It is highly complex. We both benefit immensely from one another.

X.16

I have always imagined what it was like to be a part of this world. Yet even my imagination could conjure what the last months have ensued. This world is not something I can begin to fathom. I find it both exhilarating and daunting. I observe how people perform around him. He is never wrong. They bend over backwards to make sure everything he wants, he has. His lifestyle is lavish. He has more money than he knows what to do with, rising fame, and access to anything and everything.

We stepped out to grab coffee yesterday afternoon after spending the last eight hours locked in the recording studio. I was yearning for a break. He was reluctant at first to leave, claiming we would lose all our progress. I insisted we get out, begging him not to send one of his three assistants, insinuating we should take a walk. Letting out a garrulous moan, he eventually gave in to me.

The woman who took our order almost fainted when she realized it was him. What was supposed to be a quick coffee run turned into a fan frenzy, people crying upon meeting him, elaborating with such intensity how his music changed their lives, and with me taking no less than a hundred pictures of him and his fans. I saw them acclaim him, asphyxiating him with incessant praise. Simultaneously, my admiration magnified. I became hypnotized by his esteem, utterly entranced.

The world is his, and I feel elated just to be a small part of it.

X.17

I am his muse. He studies the way my body responds to his, incessantly externalizing how to adequately make a woman cum. He fails to retain his inhibitions when we are together. He is unapologetic. It is romantic. It is full of pain. It is seductively degrading. He thrusts my sexuality to new limits, to new heights. He worships how he can make my body respond to his. He is my disciplinarian. I am his inspiration. Together we compose a fucking masterpiece.

X.18

A note he left in the kitchen:

If I tell you I
   Love
   You
   Will you promise to
   Love
   Me
   Forever?

Even if my brain is a little
   Broken?

Will you promise to accept me
   Anyways
   And
   Help me
   Get
   Better?

X. 19

Nutrition that gives you existence
   Your tongue so persistent

Fuck this milk and honey shit
   It's my soul I transmit

This is the nectar of life
   Go get my knife

My cum in your throat
   You love my pussy the most

Thank me.

X.20

He is the most masculine man I have ever met but his art is so middle sex. It is a tangle of both masculine and feminine, as if he knows what to say to charm both sexes equally yet obscenely idiosyncratically. A consummate performer, a master manipulator.

X.21

It didn't take long for him to start to share his music with me.

He writes songs and asks repeatedly for my advice. We spend days in his recording studio workshopping his music, stopping only for sex.

I am part of his process, as he often tells me, the most significant part. He values my opinion above anyone else.

I am his stimulus. It started by asking for my opinions, translating effortlessly to my writing, and becoming his.

I, without really realizing what is happening, am writing all his music.

X.22

His brain is unabridged madness. I am entranced by the way he processes the world around him. He is the most fucked up person I know, in the most alluring way possible. We spent days talking about everything and anything. He is an excellent listener. He often asks me to tell him a story. Upon finishing, he asks me to repeat the story once again, but to tell it from a different perspective. He is training me. I share my artistic soul with him. He takes it and impels it into his music.

X.23

I found someone who genuinely values me. He makes me feel not only important but also intelligent. He listens to what I have to say, like a sponge; he soaks in my words. He cherishes me. I smile, he smiles. Anything I want, he gives me. I am his princess. I play little mind games with him, and he always enthralls me when he plays back. It's our version of rousing puppy love.

Today, we played Monopoly. After, we looked at a coffee table book, "National Geographic Journeys of a Lifetime 500 of the World's Greatest Trips". I painted my fingernails, baby girl, pink, while he played guitar. We talked about dragonflies, bumble bees, and the beauty of insects. I took a nap. He answered emails. I made the bed and mumbled about miniature horses while he looked up the prices and how to care for one. He promised to buy me one once the album is done, when we both have time to care properly for it. This put me in a childlike mood. The personal trainer came, and we completed a workout together. We smoked half a joint left over from the morning. Then we showered together. He washed my hair while I giggled about the name of the soap scent. He plans to order food to be delivered to the house for dinner. He'll have me for dessert. Who knows what sort of nonsense we will get into tomorrow?

X.24

The studio is our territory. We devote ours to recording and writing. We both thrive contrastively in this environment. I can write without apprehension. He can construct and produce acoustics. We never have an unequivocal purpose when we are there. Yet, we hold ourselves accountable. We won't leave without procuring more than we started with. It doesn't have to be colossal, but whatever it is, it must evolve, not repeat.

X.25

We smoke pot incessantly. He ingests other drugs, enabling him to swallow the music. We drink when we feel it could aid us. We fuck in the bathroom when we both are frustrated with the lack of subject.

> Naturally, beautiful women grip us.
> I find satisfaction in three.
> I savor their delicacy.
> Rewarding our convolutions.

X.26

"You remind me of the ocean," he said unexpectedly, not looking up from his college-ruled notebook, he was frantically scribbling in. His left hand began to reach deep into his jeans pocket. Still fixed on this notebook, he pulled out a small but elegant, spiraling, fan-shaped cream seashell. It was three in the morning. Where did he get the shell? My mind questioned. I stared at him, confused. We had stayed up all night refining lyrics. I can't recall the last time we were apart. It has been weeks. I reason that he has had this shell for quite some time. He has planned this as a way to flatter me. He pays attention to what I say, aware of how drawn I am to water. He toyed with it for a moment before holding out his gentle tattooed arm, his blue veins pulsing. He signaled me to take the shell. He paused for another moment. "You're my Ishtar."

X.27

Today he is in a bad mood, which renders my mood.

He is revulsed. He loathes the eidolon of being famous. I think, to a great extent, it unfeignedly molests him.

We rarely go out in public because of the attention he will receive. He cannot and does not go anywhere without someone recognizing him. He is imprisoned. I see what it is doing to him. It's manslaughter. He loves it, he hates it. He wants more of it, yet none of it at the same time. He wants his exertion to be released into the world, but loathes the appraisal that chaperons it. He is a contrived creature. He describes, in color, time and time again, just how quarantining fame is. He absorbs drugs, drinks excessively...I believe that to make sense of anything at all.

X.28

Understanding the limits of a human's perception and the variable that reality plays allows one to no longer be confined by interpretation. Noticeably absent was sensory perception. We synthesized our own world, categorically psychotic and we perpetrated it contemporaneously.

X.29

The recording studio is our private celestial city—a place of unimagined blessings. The angels address us without encumbering and accepting what we create at the gates of Zion. The ecstasy of love and the agony of the artist's frustration dispatches our ruthless passions as sinners, releasing the mercy of our destructive minds. And so, we cross into an entirely new world, where impurity never enters. The palm branches sway as we declare faithful victory over the enemies of our souls. A sanctuary of eternal life... heaven.

X.30

The evil in your soul came and never went.

The glory in your madness
   Brought on by your sadness

Comes alive with the songs we write
   Within the bounds of my heart
   In the middle of the night

It's just you and me
   And the hope of what we will be

X.31

How straightforward it is to want to die before you.
   A vow, a pursuit.

X.32

The only podium we ever spar from is the studio… often, in front of an audience. We televise our show. Our fighting is an amusing spectacle. The first act starts unwittingly. He says something I don't like. He tries to tell me what to do. He makes suggestions to my work that I find offensive. I am unwilling to listen to a shred of what he utters. I don't care enough about him or our relationship to want to contort. Most of our rivalries stem from the annoyance cultivated when you're around someone too much. He always surrenders. I have never lost.

X.33

It is a dangerous love affair.
   Take your hypothesis,
   Multiply it by ten.
   That's what I am living.
   That's what we have.
   That's the only way I know how to describe it,

He holds the gun...
   A maddening, erotogenic version of Russian Roulette.

X.34

He has choreographed an exquisite woman.

I love her too, but I am not her. She lives only in our writing. She lives only in our songs. She lives only when we go to bed together. The person I truly am, he can't see. He doesn't want to change me. He wants me to be the fantasy he sings about.

I am lonely.

X.35

I was willing to stupidly relinquish everything.
  I am beside myself with this fixation.

Two years later, edited –
  I am a fucking idiot.

X.36

We have been interconnected for a while, through his songs and my lyrics. By the time mentioned, I am deliberating incessantly about him being the reason I can write. I have no rationality. I am hypnotized by the declaration of his love. I have given him the ability to extract exotic dispositions and desires. He has altered me in indescribable and extraordinary ways, and during this synchronicity, I am becoming a writer.

X.37

The elevation to which he dispatches romance is unimaginable. He is a prevalent sentimentalist. He fully compels me with his eccentric romantic gestures. He devotes time and energy to creating the fairy tale I have inevitably fantasized. I never express these childlike conceptions to him. I don't have to. He cognized any method of making a woman feel loved. He lets these performances speak for themselves.

My hair was perfect.
  My makeup was perfect.
  My shoes were perfect.
  My nails were perfect.
  My body was perfect.
  My smile was perfect.
  My dress was perfect.
  The room was perfect.
  The candles were perfect.
  The food was perfect.
  The wine was perfect.
  The music was perfect.
  The conversation was perfect.
  The kiss was perfect.
  The bed was perfect.
  The sheets were perfect.
  The sex was perfect.

He was perfect. I was perfect. It was perfect.

In the morning, I recognized the disappointment of fornicating with one's fantasy.

Perfect, it turns out, is lifeless.

X.38

A leech is a happy companion without a clue of the damage it induces. The leech's bite causes a direct connection between its body and the host's body.

Feeding itself, the leech sucks the hosts' blood.

The ignorant leech doesn't know it is killing the host.
Can you blame the leech?

X.39

What started as a love affair has deformed into what now feels like work. The sparkle of lust dimmed to a faint light of obligation. My sense of independence has all but evaporated under the heat of our progressed relationship. Spending every second of everyday with him is grueling. I fantasize about what and who is next. The more I push, the more he pulls. He knows things between us are changing. The relationship has stalled.

X.40

In the deepest trenches, love is found
  Stimulated moans, the only sound

He wanders the obscure streets at dawn
  Apprehensively praying she isn't gone

Suicide is easy, he said
  Right before he bled

The funeral was beautiful; everyone was there
  She, of course, did not care

X.41

"I can't do this anymore," I said.
"I know," he replied.

X.42

The end hasn't been filled with hate. It wasn't my idea, it wasn't his. The relationship ended as naturally as it started. We had a healthy relationship. We were both mature about the breakup. The love we had was infatuation. I knew it, and so did he. It was four months of paradise. He must go to a new city. I have no desire to go with him. I want to be free to live my dreams, and he needs to go pursue his. We agreed not to speak, to not contact each other. We both want a clean break. My intentions are pure. Leaving this relationship, I believe that I have gained more than I lost. I feel satisfied about saying goodbye. I feel that we have both changed each other for the better. It is time to move on. We have no more to offer each other. It has been the most amicable breakup I have ever had. I am not sad. I am at peace.

X.43

We took advantage of our time together. We were inseparable. Spending days locked in various hotel rooms and recording studios, working to tap into each other's potential. He saw something in me that the others had failed to see. He fell in love with my potential. There was stability in the relationship that I liked - we worked more like business partners than anything. It was a restorative, transparent love, and I flourished creatively.

X.44

As the days, months, and years passed, I remember our time together tenderly. I started to write my first novel, and he continued his success in the music industry. I never spoke about our affair. I never felt the need to. I never mention his name to anyone. There is a part of me that wholeheartedly enjoys keeping him a secret. I respect his privacy. I respect his wishes. I never wanted to tell anyone. I don't want my name to be attached to his.

My ego would never allow it.

X.45

It had been approaching two years since the last time we had seen each other. It was a depressingly cold day when I finally heard. I knew of his success— everyone in the world knows of his success—but it was a depressingly cold day in Chicago when I heard him singing my words, my songs—mine.

I was in thorough disbelief. It took me nearly a month to comprehend what he had done to me.

He shattered everything.
He stole the thing that meant the most to me and told everyone it was his.

All I know is how to write.
The words I was most proud of were stolen.

X.46

Did you do what you did so I wouldn't forget you? Would your ego feel better if I called you? Are you still waiting for my reaction?

You don't want me to forget you & you won't let yourself forget me.

It's a mortifyingly embarrassing attempt to get someone's attention, don't you think?

X.47

It all makes sense, why you can't keep a girlfriend, why you can't stay in one city, why you spend all your time working, and why you drink the whole bottle. You know what you did, you know you stole something from me. I heard your songs, but we both know those are my words. You must keep running from everyone you deceive. Strangers worship you because they accredit my words to you.

Your life is based on deception.
   You are nothing more than a very good liar.
   The only valuable thing about you is everything I left behind.

X.48

Fuck your NDA
    I am going to write about you anyway
    And that Grammy nomination
    It's a shame they didn't have all the information
    All the songs I wrote with you
    If only everyone knew
    How does it feel to be a fraud?
    What will happen when everyone knows you're flawed
    Don't worry, I'll never tell
    Never about the nights I spent writing in your hotel
    You must think about me every day
    Every time you hit play
    I often wonder how you sleep at night
    Terrified I might one day write
    Yet, up until today
    I never had much to say
    But I think it's time to address
    The secret behind your success
    All your number one songs
    My name is the one that belongs
    Let me help you recall
    That I am the one who wrote them all

X.49

I often contemplate how different my life might be if he had given me the writer's credit that I deserved. Where would I be? Would I, instead of writing this book, be in a recording studio writing music? Would some sort of acknowledgement make the circumstances better? What did I need to feel composed again? Would anyone even believe me?

There were and still aren't any answers to these questions. I inherently concluded that by doing nothing, I was doing something.

I have never cried about it.

I have never thought of getting a lawyer and proceeding to get some sort of redemption.

I have never wished ill upon him.

I have never told anyone who he is and what we mean to each other.

I have never spoken a word of this transgression to anyone, not even those closest to me.

I have never cared enough to pick up the phone when he calls.

I moved on from him, that part of my life, those words, my songs, that art, and the worst betrayal of my life.

X. 50

I sleep just fine at night, knowing I am his worst fear.
   And there is nothing more powerful than being feared.
   You never want a Scorpio as an enemy.

X.51

& what is fear, but an unpleasant emotion caused by the belief that someone or something is dangerous, likely to cause pain, or a threat.

& what is your greatest threat, but indisputable evidence?

- The laptop
- The hard drive
- The hours of video
- The hundreds of photos
- The recordings of the sessions in the studio
- The handwritten notes
- The witnesses

The burden of proof.

How to Turn a Boy Into a Man

Part three:

This is a unique circumstance, for the lessons on how to teach this boy to be a man have yet to be learned. If you somehow find yourself in a similar circumstance, you must continue to have unquestioned faith in karmic retribution. Some lessons are not bound by time, only to the exact right circumstance. A boy will believe that you forgot about the wrongdoings, moved on, maybe even forgave him. However, a man knows that a lesson taught through the vengeance of a wronged woman is the most impactful omen. Some say the best revenge is none at all, not me though, the best revenge has still yet to come, this chronicle is only the beginning…

These lessons, coupled with others found later in this book, will aid in teaching a boy to be a man.

G

27 years old

The almost love of my life.

G.1

It was the closest revelation to love at first sight that I have ever known.
From the moment I saw him, I imagined he would change my life.
I will never forget the first time I laid eyes on him.

He was the most beautiful boy I had ever seen. I discovered him somnolently sitting by the unlit campfire, near the center of the hostel. It was the only place with working WIFI for miles, and there he was, gazing down at his iPhone. His coiled light brown hair was half pulled back, his golden hooped nose ring shining perfectly alongside the gleam of the day. His elbows pressed into his thighs as he sat hunched over, smoking a hand-rolled cigarette. I studied him. He inhaled the smoke slowly and with intention, exhaled with ease. He was flirting with his facial hair, running his soft, masculine hands from his cheeks to his chin, brushing his beard as he continued to be fixated on the phone. In a dirty white cut-off tank top and jean shorts, he sat on the edge of the log, happily oblivious. I couldn't refrain from gaping at him; there was something advantageously sexy about him, this enigmatical traveler.

I perpetually deliberate if it was a measure of destiny that we met in front of the fire in the forests of South Africa, for this day changed the course of our lives forever. I believe now, more than ever, that soulmates will find their way to each other, and it comes when you think it is impossible for you ever to love again.

A year later...

To read a great love story is one thing, but to live it is a transcendent experience, prevailing over all realities. Meeting in Africa, my intuition knew that my heart had been pursuing him for all this time. I undoubtedly met him. I have found the person I am going to spend the rest of my life with. He is my soulmate.

Three years later...

I was wrong, catastrophically wrong.

G.2

Subsequently, that same night, we found ourselves dancing, covered in a blanket of stars while singing along to the Eagles. In the midst of that mid-June summer evening, I decided I needed more of him. Up until this point, we hadn't spent much time together. We had spoken, but I knew no Hebrew, and his broken English didn't get us far. The fact that he was a stranger didn't matter to me. I had no idea who he was, why he was here, or if he had any interest in me at all. I didn't care. I don't know how to explain it, other than I just knew, perhaps you could call it intuition. Something inside me told me I needed him. That night I had him.

The next morning, I left without giving him my number, without saying goodbye. I later uncovered the lengths he went to get into contact with me. He was exhausting every resource available to get my number. His text came too late. By the time I received it, I was gone with no intention of returning.

G.3

Living in my rental car, I have been driving my way through Namibia and up into Botswana for the past few weeks. We haven't spoken, but he hasn't disappeared from my imagination. I was left deprived of knowing more about this beautiful boy. I left because I thought I had gotten everything I needed from him. I was so fiercely mistaken. Why won't he leave my mind? Fanatical thoughts. It's an... illustrious amalgamation of attraction and fascination.

There comes a time in your life when you are compelled to take a chance, when you must follow the pursuit of your heart. I understand that this... impetuosity is something more, something so powerful that I can't escape it. I must surrender.

Tonight, in the middle of Africa, I will use what little data I have purchased to text him. I am intent on not making our night in South Africa the last time that I see him.

G.4

I have been living in and volunteering at a diminutive orphanage outside of Livingston, Zambia. A month or so has passed since he and I were in tandem. We have begun to talk every day, sending voice messages to each other indefatigably. I spend hours probing and analyzing each and every part of our conversations, trying to derive messages to send him. I overthink everything, but I can't help it. I want him to like me. I am roused, yearning to auscultate. Like a young girl with a crush, I am fundamentally infatuated. Fundamentally, an infatuated girl can't be held responsible for their actions.

It's arousing to pursue someone new; it has been years since I was captivated by another person. Almost too engrossed, I must know everything about him. How can I learn everything about him through WhatsApp? It is unreasonable.

Two weeks we have passed since we communicated again. I invited him to come see me in Zambia, but he is traveling with his friends, and he can't abandon them. In his next breath, he invited me to travel with himself and his group of friends in Mozambique.

The curiosity that has been brought on by these conversations and my illustrious imagination has driven me to buy the ticket. My whole being thirsts for this. I can't explain it. It is the behavior of someone brain-sick. It is the most ludicrous thing I have ever done, to fly across the continent to see a boy I barely know. We have spent less than 48 hours together.

Life doesn't happen to you; you take it.
I have no idea what I am getting into.
My heart tingles.
I am buying the ticket on a feeling deep in my heart.
I am going to see him again.

G.5

Essentially, we were two strangers only a week ago; now we behave as though we have been in a relationship for years. In the morning, we wake up and make love. He goes to buy eggs, tomatoes, drinking water, and bread from the market. He cooks me breakfast while I shower. We eat together. I clean the kitchen. I get dressed and ready for the day. We make love again. I make the bed. He showers. We laugh. He sings. He smokes cigarettes. We put on sunscreen. We go to the beach. We go to scuba diving school. We swim in the ocean. We smoke a joint. We see our friends. We eat again. We smile. We enjoy another beautiful day in Tofu Beach. We do not have one worry in the world. The coastline is phenomenal. We often spot Humpback Whales swimming right off the shore. Our friends are all sharing a small beachfront Airbnb for the next week. We have the master bedroom. The bed and the windows face directly to the ocean. It is paradise.

We are progressively getting to know each other. I have acquired a substantial amount of information about him, which compels me to want to gain more. We hail from opposite sides of the world. A notion I am transfixed by. We don't have to force anything when we are together, our connection comes innately. My soulmate.

G.6

I am lying on our bed in Mozambique, a small hut by the beach, a five-minute walk from our previous Airbnb. We have been living here for close to a week, for no more than twelve dollars a night. It is minuscule, one room, just large enough for two people to comfortably stand. Our bed is draped with a mosquito net. One nightstand crowded with several small items dominates the room. The sheets are a deep shade of blue. The ground is frigid. Our backpacks and what they contain are methodically placed in the far-right back corner. We don't have many simple travelers.

I customarily write lying on the bed. In the short time we have known each other, he can easily comprehend how important this time is for me. I am left alone with my pen and paper while he smokes his hand-rolled cigarettes with the others outside, adjacent to the fire pit, a few minutes' walk from our hut.

Twenty minutes later…

He swung open the hut door and saw me writing. At first, I didn't look up, assuming he was coming to retrieve something he had forgotten. The only sound was my pen dancing across the paper. I continued to write as he just stared at me. His brown eyes fixed ardently on what I was doing.

I looked up. Immediately, without hesitation, he came towards me. He began to undress me, pulling off my shirt, exposing my breasts, slipping my underwear gently down my legs, kissing my inner thighs as we locked eyes. He fucked me intensely, with such a delicate force, until we both came.

After, I lay naked, catching my breath, awestricken at what just happened. While he was getting dressed, pulling his yellow sweatshirt over his head, he stared at me assertively and said, "There, now you have something to write about."

It's the most romantic thing anyone has ever done for me.

G.7

As you take hold of my hips
  Transcribing profound devotion
  Penetrating previously unseen emotions
  I ache to write poems
  On your skin
  With my lips
  Endless love scripts

G.8

My writing has become centered around him and us. I have sequentially inaugurated him as my muse. Once I trigger the writing of a person, for a person, with a person in mind, I become maddened with them. I fell in love with him on both the page and in reality.

I don't know the exact moment that I knew I was falling in love with him. It is happening with a tender patience; every day, I become more and more encapsulated, not just with him, but with everything he does. I find myself watching him all the time. I want to see how he reciprocates the world. He operates euphorically. The world doesn't move around him; he moves with the world. It is angelic.

The intimacy he elicits is an affair of our hearts. Where I lack in particular prowess, he atones for them. He nourishes me in ways that I never knew possible. We were two strangers who had been propelled into a relationship. To call it a relationship doesn't give it justice to what we have authored. It is devotion. We have moved as quickly as wildfire. We have incinerated without hesitation, becoming a collaborative conflagration. We are living my most desirous fantasy – traveling the world while falling in love.

G.9

I don't know if we're alone in the universe
   But it feels like the world is ours
   Tonight, tomorrow, and every day after
   Time doesn't exist when I am with him
   No, I won't let this feeling go
   Love is where our summer is

        This is what it is to be happy.

G.10

"You're gonna love it," I said.
  "What?" He replied.
  "The world."

G.11

We have spent this month in Mozambique falling in love. He explicates the meaning of intimacy. We have an impenetrable connection. The transparency we built is restorative. It feels safe to be open with him. I have never had a relationship quite like him and I. We have moved without complications. We can't get enough of each other. It is an occult interval.

However, we both know it will only last a few more days. We aren't permitted to stay any longer in Mozambique with our visas. I am going to Tanzania to volunteer, and he is going back to Cape Town to incur life. Our time together is bleakly running out. I am sad.

G.12

The bed is lugubrious without his body next to mine.

The weeks we have spent apart have been grueling. After parting ways in Mozambique, I can't help but sense that a diminutive part of me is absent. I long for him. I miss him desperately. He rarely leaves my mind, almost to the point of mental exhaustion. My heart is in flames. We have kept communicating, but it isn't substantial, only talking every couple of days or so.

      I pray to every God to bring us back to one another.

G. 13

I am leaving the school tomorrow. I have reached my goal, raising enough money to give the school running water and complete various other renovations. I feel as though I have accomplished all I can here. I have more of Africa that I want to journey through. I will take a night train to Arusha and begin climbing Mount Kilimanjaro tomorrow. With that in mind, I have decided we both should move on. We must not communicate anymore. I chose to end our relationship, letting him know that it is senseless and torturous for us to keep talking. I want to trek this mountain, summit, and descend with the hopes of a new start. I must let go. We are just destined for travelers' love and nothing more.

One week later...
After climbing the mountain-

I turned my phone on for the first time in a week. He bought a plane ticket. He is coming to spend a month with me in Zanzibar. I can't believe it. I will see him in less than a week.

G.14

We spent many of those days on the island off the coast of Tanzania, falling madly in love. We would lie in bed, a little longer than usual, for we had nothing to do but lavish the days on this island with each other. He would wake me every morning with sex and fresh mango juice. When we would finally get out of bed, he would drink his morning coffee, and together we would slowly make our way through the morning, just the two of us with a harmonious silence in the air. We did everything together – showering, eating, laughing, exploring, sleeping, playing, fighting, dancing, swimming, crying. We would swim naked in the warm, crystal blue ocean together almost every day. We make love in the ocean, on the beach, in public, in the bathroom, in the shower, on the bed, in the open – everywhere and anywhere. I think that's my favorite feeling in the world. We were never apart, and I never wanted to be. I spent those idyllic days with him, only him, with not a single worry on our minds, and a sort of peace in the atmosphere that comes with truly finding your forever, finding your true love.

G.15

Occasionally, we fight.
    Culturally, we clash.
    Our age difference plays a factor.
    Money causes disputes.
    Too much time together ensues annoyance.
    He will say mean words to me.
    I will try to control him.

But we always make up, no matter what, no matter what.

G.16

Outside myself, I dwell upon my heart every time I see him.
He is the person who looked at me with nothing but pure and genuine
tenderness.
He was a melody the universe wrote to reintroduce me to what being loved
should feel like.

G.17

The last month has been as close to perfect as I have ever encountered. I want to stay here forever, just him and I on this island, living in perfect bliss. We have almost entirely disconnected from the world outside this island. After all this time, we have engineered a routine here – our beloved coffee spots, which bars to go to on which nights, making friends with other expats, and learning the language. I tell him, we can find jobs here, start a life, run away together, and never return. This is what I want, but this is not reality. In two days, he is leaving. His money ran out. He must go back to Israel. His after-army travels have come to an end. He must go to college, find a job, and figure out what he wants to do with his life. This chapter of our adventure together is over. Once again, he must leave me, but we have made a plan. We will meet again in Egypt, our fourth country together, in just a few weeks.

He has become part of me in such a way that I don't know how I will endure time without him.

G.18

You are gone
   Traveled on
   To universes far away
   Beyond my display
   But I smile
   For awhile
   Reliving the night
   You gave me a reason to write

G.19

I have traveled the world
  Sailed the seven seas
  Just for the universe to bring you to me.

One more week until I see him again.

G.20

We have been reunited in Egypt.

He adores my now bleach blonde hair. I bought brand new clothes in Cairo so he could see me in something other than the five original outfits I have been traveling with. I only have room for so much in my backpack, not allowing for variety. I got baby pink press on nails to wear and I painted my toenails white. I want him to think I am beautiful. I want to look beautiful for him.

We are staying in a lovely, white stone cottage near the rocky Red Sea beach. We play backgammon for hours, teaching me Hebrew numbers. We drink, eat, and laugh. He always makes me laugh. I cry laughing so hard. He fucks me whenever and wherever he pleases. We are religiously having sex, at a minimum, three times a day. I am addicted. At any given moment, he bursts out singing parts of English songs, more often than not, getting the lyrics wrong. He is forever touching me, pulling me into him, kissing me all the time, brushing my hair away from my face, and placing his hand on my thighs. I am not accustomed to affection. He loves to touch me.

We climbed up the mountain today to watch the sunset over the Red Sea. Earlier today, we went snorkeling together. Two of his friends came from Israel to join us. I love them, too. Now, I know all his best friends, the six of them, with their matching ass tattoos.

He got me a gift, a gold Star of David necklace. I wear it close to my heart. I will never take it off. It will protect me. It's my most cherished item because he gave it to me. It is my favorite thing in the world, besides him.

G.21

On my knees
  Give me your offering, please.

Sunday service
  Pleasuring you is my purpose.

I'll do anything you need
  Please, baby, allow my mouth your seed.

It's an honor to fulfill your desires
  Doing anything you require.

G. 22

The sex we have is something else entirely.
   I have never felt something so powerful – a mesmerizing heaven.
   I am ensorcelled.
   It is love.

G.23

He is my soulmate, my partner, the love of my life.
   Life makes sense when I am with him.
   He taught me to believe in true love and happily ever after.
   I exhausted my unbroken life searching for him.
   We are two souls connected.
   People allocate their whole lives to find what I found in you.
   I see my future, our future -

And when I avowed that I loved him, I realized that assuredly, I had never loved anyone before.

I love you for all that you are, all that you have been, and all that you are yet to be.

G.24

He gets frustrated with me.
He has never been so intertwined with an artist.
He can't grasp it.
He wishes to read my writing.
Immensely so, it is causing massive arguments.
He has admitted to taking my journal and reading it when I was not
looking.

It brings him irritation to be out of this part of my life.
It brings him disappointment to see me write and not allow him access to it.
It brings him dreadful curiosity.

You are my art.
You are the sanity.
You are the purpose.

You are, without exception, the hero of this novel.

G.25

Everything I am seeking to write
　Everything I am failing to articulate

Trying to piece together the authentic words
　Toying unceasingly with complex expressions

　　　　　　　All to simply say I love my lips between your legs.

G.26

Our travels in Egypt have come to an end. Again, we must separate. Again, we must say goodbye. Again, I feel that it will be the last time I see him. We tried desperately to find a way for me to go back with him to Israel. It is impossible. Impossible because I don't have the vaccine. Impossible because there is no way for me to get the vaccine. Impossible for us to be together. Impossible.

The torment of falling in love.

We cried together as we said our last goodbyes, watching the sun gaze upon the Red Sea. Unable to stop the tears from flowing, I told him how much he changed my life, how proud I am of him, how he can do anything in this world, how I will miss him forever.

When the bus arrived, I cried the whole way back to Cairo. Devastated to lose him once again.

G.27

We were happy, we were happy, and the universe punished us for it. It took you away from me.

We are a world apart. I don't know if I will ever see you again. I have never felt such mournful sorrow. After eight months, I left Africa to head to Southeast Asia. I will arrive in Cambodia tonight. There is no more plan to be together again. Fate has it that we are to be separate from each other. It feels symbolic to finally leave Africa, like it's the start of a new chapter and the end of our great love story.

G.28

I miss you, and I cannot find any more words to tell you how much this hurts. To be apart from you and it's beyond our control to be together. The distance between us appears colossal. It grows, dreadful feelings steadily taking control of me, hastily and powerless. You are the endeavor of my humanity. I lie awake during the silent hours of the night. I contemplate calling him every night we are apart and telling him.

I can't sleep without him.
I can't live without him.
I can't exist without him.

G.29

We haven't seen each other in months. After nearly a year of traveling, I am finally going back to the United States. The year of traveling the world and he was the best thing to come out of it. We still talk every day. We haven't given up on each other. I don't know how, when, or if I will ever see him again. I am torn between fighting for him and starting a new life, without him.

I feel tortured.
   Please, don't do it
   Don't love me
   Unable to surrender to stability
   Someone like me must be free

G.30

Four months later...
New York City

2 AM
  I wrote my vows tonight, for when we get married.
  They just came to me.
  They are the most poetic words I've ever composed.

3 AM
  I can't be without him. I can't. I bought a ticket to Israel.

G.31

Haim Sheli.

G.32

I knew I loved him from the second I saw him. I knew he would be the one to change my life.

I knew I was never going to be the same person. I knew when I met him, that I was somehow reborn to a different version of myself. He gave me a second life.

When you find it, you'll know it. It doesn't happen overnight. It doesn't happen in an instant. It's unsystematic. It's dactylic. It's the single most intrinsic thing to ensue in a person. To love someone, to really fucking love someone. It's divine intervention. When you fall in love, you conceive it, you delve into it, you draw breath from it.

Love inhabits you. It's the meaning of life.

G.33

I bought the ticket as a declaration of my love, my devotion. We want this relationship. We want this to work. I have never felt this way about anyone else. It must be a sign, a sign to fight for us. It is a big step in the right direction, it's a lot of sacrifice, but he is worth it. We spent time apart and on multiple occasions ended the relationship. We stopped talking, we tried to move on, but it didn't work; we always came back to each other. During this time, I thought about staying in New York, but there was nothing for me in America. I don't need a visa to enter Israel. He needs someone to come to the United States. Easy, I didn't give leaving again a second thought. My family and friends understand. They see how happy we make each other. I love showing him off, posting pictures together, and confessing to all my friends how happy I am to be in love. They encourage me to pursue our relationship. The only thing my friends and family want is to meet the boy who finally stole my heart. We both see a future together, and a future together means I must go to him. I am spending the next six weeks living with him in Jerusalem.

G.34

It has been harder than I thought adjusting to life in Israel. We are living in
an Airbnb I rented for us in the center of the city now, but the first week
we spent living in the house he grew up in with his mom and dad. They are
nothing but sweet and kind to me. His brothers, sisters, nieces, and nephews
have all been welcoming. Communication with them and people here in
general is difficult. I don't speak, read, or write Hebrew. Although English
is spoken here, often things get lost in translation. No one understands my
references or my accent. When we are with his friends, they all, of course,
speak Hebrew. I usually remain quite next to him. I am there, but mostly
I am in my head. I spend a lot of time trapped in silence. I rely on him to
communicate for me. The buildings and houses are unlike what I am used
to; they are smaller, older, and made from different materials. The country
is tiny; it seems everyone knows everyone. The music is new to me, too. It
is mostly trance music that I have a hard time connecting with and dancing
to. Everyone I know, I know through him. I have no friends of my own
here. Israel is not a theocracy, but it feels as though it is. This is something
I am not used to, so much religion everywhere. Religion brings conflict.
I like the food. I don't mind eating kosher and shakshuka. I miss pork. I
don't look like the other girls here. They have dark and curly hair. I have
blonde and straight hair. They have dark eyes. I have light. They are short.
I am tall. They wear black. I wear color. The clothes in America are far
more revealing than the ones here; my clothes make me stand out. He hates
my American clothes. The lifestyle is foreign too. My everyday life here is
not what I expected. He is enrolled in a college course and working on his

schoolwork all the time. Young adults go to college in America; in Israel, they go into the army and then start college. We are in contrasting phases of life. When he isn't working on school, he shows me all around Israel. We borrow his dad's car and go on little adventures. He is very proud of his country. I found an aerial studio close by. It is my happy place. He showed me how to get there using the city's public bus. I go to take classes at night. It is my therapy. I am happy, but it has been challenging. I can't tell him how difficult it has been for me. He is doing everything he can to accommodate me and make me feel welcome and comfortable in this faraway place. I figure I am just going through an intense culture shock that will wear off in time. I wonder how he would adjust if it were the other way around. What if he came to America? I keep telling myself that none of that matters because I am with him. I can envision what it would be like to spend our lives together. We aren't traveling anymore, we are living. It is a glimpse of what my future with him would be.

G.35

I loved him before we had a name for it.
   I am in love with him.
   I am going to marry him.
   I am going to be the mother of his children.
   I am going to love him for the rest of our lives.

G.36

I didn't really notice it at first. I was so infatuated with him. I didn't realize what my brain was unconsciously doing. He said that Instagram was the worst thing about me, so I stopped using Instagram. He always wanted to see and touch my body, so it became the most valuable thing to me. He wanted access to things that I didn't necessarily want to share with him, but I shared them anyway. He told me that as his girlfriend, I needed to give him what he wanted, and it was "sad" that I couldn't be more open with him. I didn't realize at first that I was losing myself for him. He didn't love me purely. He loved me for who he could mold me to be. He needed me to be Jewish, he wanted me to keep my blonde hair, he wanted me to cover my body, and he was making decisions for us. Honestly, I didn't care. I was just happy to be with him. None of these changes seemed to make that much of a difference in my life. They seemed so small. I truly didn't notice until I did.

"You will have to change if you see a future with us."

He did want to change me.
It had become so clear.
I didn't want to change.
I love who I am.
It was devastating to learn that he didn't.

G.37

We took the train to Tel Aviv today.
He took me to the modern art museum, which is one of my favorite things
to do.
I loved the whole day, I loved the art, I loved being there.
I appreciate art, really appreciate it.
He told me it was stupid.
He couldn't see the beauty.
I cried on the train ride home.

G.38

I knew he was incredibly insecure for a long time.
He couldn't handle a woman like me.
He couldn't handle my confidence.
He couldn't handle that I refused to make myself smaller to appeal to his
ego.
I threatened him.

G.39

We broke up.
    I don't want it anymore.
    He begged me to stay with him.
    I didn't want to.
    I can't explain it, but sometimes,
    He makes me hate myself.
    I can't bring myself to tell him,
    Because I'd never want to hurt his feelings.
    I am heading to Ukraine without him.

G.40

It had been about two months since we last saw each other. I completed my volunteer work on the border between Ukraine and Poland, doing my part to help with the war. Now, I am backpacking through Eastern Europe. He refuses to leave me alone, begging to be together again. He doesn't want to give up on us. He is so sure that he wants to be together. I need time to think. I am torn on what I want. Do I still love him? Is it time to move on?

I decided to block his number and give myself space and time to clear my head.

A week later, somewhere in Bulgaria, I was out one night drinking with my friends. I decided to unblock his number because it was time to talk, to figure things out, and to have an honest conversation about our future, which he was so sure we would have together.

"Drink as you can now. Soon you cannot drink"
"Why"
"Because you're going to be pregnant."
"Don't say that unless you mean it."
"I love you and I want to spend my life with you. You are the girl of my life. The time that we didn't talk made me realize this."
"Why"
"I missed you. I understand that you are the woman who changed my life. I understand that after you, there is nothing for me."

Less than five minutes later, he confessed over text that within the week I had blocked his number, he had met a girl on Tinder, had sex with her in the back of his dad's car, and was sorry. He said that being with another girl made him realise how important I was to him. This wasn't the first time something like this had happened. It was just the first time he was honest about it. Once again, he broke my heart.

G.41

He flew to Albania to save our relationship.
It worked, I forgave him for being with another girl, even though it broke
me.
We had disgusting sex for four days nonstop.
We fell back in love.

We vacationed in Greece.
It was a fairytale.
We danced together under the moonlight.
Shibari.

I am heading back to Israel in two weeks.
His personal pornstar.

G.42

He ignites every atom in my body.

The way he wants to pleasure me is so effective. I couldn't remain alive without his tongue savoring my flesh. Our sex drives are indistinguishably parallel. There isn't a place, time, or position we don't want to fuck from. He takes control and unmercifully, I do everything he wants. It is a fusion of unguarded, vulgar, erotic fucking.

I am so powerful when I am on top of him.
The energy we transmitted together was transcendent.
He unveils my authority.

G.43

I love you, baby.

G.44

The days in Jerusalem are spent with ease. I have adjusted to life here. In the last year, I have spent more time in Israel than even my own country. This city feels like home. I love it here. I am slowly accepting that this could be my new home, our home.

He has become less controlling. We seem to be in a better place. We have started to talk more seriously about our future. I am five years older than he is. We want the same things. I just want them much quicker than he does. I want to be married, I want to have children, I want to move on to this next chapter in my life. He is only 23, and while he wants these things, part of me feels like I am stealing his youth by putting these demands on him. He doesn't have an education, no career, and no money. He has yet to have the time to establish himself. How can he provide for me? For us? The things I want in life, he is not there yet, and I don't know what that means for our future. Still, every time I wake up, I love him even more than the day before.

G.45

He loved my body.
  He worshiped my body.
  He undressed my body.
  He was inside my body.
  He touched my body.
  He absorbed my body.
  He studied my body.
  He took videos of my body.
  He owned my body.

He loved me because of my body, if only for my body.

He established my body as the utmost imperative thing in his world,
And I hate him for it.

G.46

I saw the way he loved me. The devotion he had. The way he was willing to overlook everything and anything just to be with me. Driving himself mad trying to keep me. Even when he learned all my secrets, able to stand in front of me and love me, and I knew this love. I recognized what was happening. I saw my life, there with him, it was perfect. He loved me. He loved me more than anyone else ever had. I saw the house, the kids, the future, and forever. I was so close I could touch, taste, grasp it in my hands, feeling every pulse of the life we could make together.

> The life that never happened,
> My life with him, my beautiful boy.

G.47

And in the end, what it really came down to is the music he loved, I hated
  & his utter lack of oral hygiene.

G.48

It's over, it's finally over.
    It is just not going to work.
    We broke up on FaceTime last night.
    There is nothing more I can say about it.
    I am back here in New York, and he is there.
    We live in two different worlds.
    I can't do it anymore.
    The things I need from him, I will never get.
    How did I ever think we would be together forever?
    How was I such a fool?
    A beautiful thing is rarely perfect.

G.49

It was just too complicated to work.

Emotionally, we were in two different places. We were on two different timelines. The saying, "right person, wrong time," always rings in my head when I think of our relationship. We had both made mistakes in the relationship. While I loved him enough to forgive him, he couldn't do the same for me. The logistics of belonging to two very contrasting parts of the world played a role. Money, time, and age contributed to our eventual end. We didn't stop loving each other. We both just sort of gave up, or so I thought.

G.50

Almost is the hardest way to be loved by someone.

He almost loved me.
I almost loved him.
We almost got married.
We almost had children.
We almost grew old together.
We almost spent the rest of our lives together.
He was almost my soulmate.
We almost had everything.

Almost.

G.51

I was stupidly willing to sculpt my whole life around him. I wanted it. I wanted him and us more than anything in this world. I wanted our relationship to triumph with every ounce of love I could generate.

It failed.

& in the end, this caused me nothing but formidable sorrow.
Taking months to rehabilitate from, to mourn.
Crying myself to sleep with notions of him moving on, forgetting about me and us.
Reaching out, hoping he still loved me, too.
Only to get left more broken.

G.52

This breakup devastated me.
  I devoted everything to the relationship.
  I truly never loved anyone the way I loved him.

It was my money that was paying for all the flight tickets -his and mine, the Airbnb's, food, groceries, everything we did. I showered him with trips, traveling, dinners, expensive wine, and experiences for over a year. I was financially paying for everything. He never paid. Not for one thing. He was upset with the reason I had money, but when it came time to spend it, the problems disappeared. I came to his country, time after time, because he couldn't come to mine. I took the 12-hour flights. I put my life on hold. I changed my life to make it work. I was completely integrated into his life. His friends were my friends. I knew them all. I traveled with most of them. I knew his family. I loved his family. I knew his country, language, religion, and culture. I experienced his life so intimately, and he never even briefly encountered mine. I was substantially more committed than he was.

I sacrificed everything, and he never thanked me.
  He never appreciated everything I did for him, for us.

I didn't want to see our relationship fail. I didn't want our perfect love story to miscarry.

There were times he was cruel to me. He would get mad and call me names.

"Slut.", "Whore." He would tell me I was stupid. He told me no one would ever love me, that I would be a horrible mother. No matter how mad I was at him, I never said a malicious thing to him. I wasn't perfect, and I made mistakes too, but I never tried to hurt him intentionally. He called what I did going to "stripper class," but I've never taken my clothes off. He would make comments on what I wore or how the skin on my face looked. We would break up, and within days, he would be with other women. I had to forgive him, even when I wasn't ready. At the time, I didn't care about any of it because I was in love with him.

And this is the love that I thought would last forever.

The person I invested my heart & soul into, the person I was going to spend the rest of my life with, continue to travel the world with, have a family with, the person I would die next to.

I watched him walk out of my life as if it were the easiest thing he had ever done.

As quickly as it started, the fairytale came to an end.

G.53

Can you imagine your life where I don't exist?
  Don't worry.
  Soon you will live it.

G.54

Six months after the breakup -

I begged for him back.
 I begged for our relationship.
 I begged for one more chance.
 I broke up with him, and I started to regret it.

I fear I will never find what we had again.
 I fear that I didn't try hard enough and that I gave up too soon.
 I fear that I lost the love of my life.
 I fear that I will live with this regret until the day I die.

Am I romanticizing the suffering?

G.55

We are meeting in India.

I have to see him again.
  I have to tell him everything I feel.
  I need him to look me in the eyes and tell me it's really over.
  I need him to tell me it is all in my head, that he isn't my person.
  I need him to tell me that he fell out of love with me.
  I need him to tell me that I have to move on.
  I need to say goodbye.

G. 56

Currently, I am reluctant to include this page.
However, I must.
If you know who G is, I request that you do not read.
I allowed myself to be treated this way.
I do not believe that people should be judged by one single moment in life.
I toyed for months with including this page.
Please read with grace, as we have all made mistakes.

———————————————————

I was broken. I was lost.
    Mostly, I was desperate.
    I needed to see him in India.

He demanded that the only way he would see me was if I sent him naked pictures and videos of myself, touching myself for him. This and only this was the way that he would "make time" for me. He blackmailed me. I didn't want to, I hate doing it, but that is the power he had over me. Screaming on the phone to leave him alone unless I sent my body. Demanding that they "were the best videos I could send." "Be a pornstar." That this was the only way he would consider seeing me. That he was going to block me forever unless I sent a number of pictures and multiple videos.

I was so poisoned with love, of course, I did it.

I was humiliated during and after.
To this day, the closest I've ever felt to suicide.
For days, in the very literal sense, he made me want to kill myself.
I felt worthless.
I felt used.
I felt nothing and everything.

How could someone I love so deeply do this to me? My soulmate?

I should have known then and there.

To this day, this is the worst thing another human being has done to me.
I cry writing this page.
I cry for that little girl, who only wanted to be loved.
There is a special place in hell for him.
There is a special place in hell for me for forgiving him.

G.57

It has been one month since I flew to India to see him.
 We spent four days together, and it was like nothing had changed.
 We were perfect together.

The answers I needed, I found:
 Without a doubt in my mind, I love him.
 Without a doubt in my mind, we are not meant to be together forever.

To see him one last time, to say goodbye in India, was what my heart needed, and my soul had longed for these last six months. I no longer stay up at night wondering "what if". It was finally finished in both my mind and reality.

> At last, I thought, I could release him.
> I can fall out of love.
> Or so I thought.

G.58

Months passed. I was in New York. He moved to Australia.

We tried as best as we could to stay away from each other. Failing every time, coming back to each other time and time again. We fell in love all over again. We spent the better part of nine months in a relationship via WhatsApp. I urged him to invite me there, to start our lives, to finally give us a real shot. We both felt it, this cosmic unification. It was more superior than love. We wanted to move on from each other, but simply put, the universe had other plans. It seemed every time we tried to forget, the love was too powerful, too strong, too pure. It pulled us back to one another. We were going to end up together. I knew, I knew deep down, we were meant to be together. That all the bullshit didn't matter. I made mistakes. He did, too. What is love but a form of ultimate forgiveness? It was him. It was always him. He was my forever. He was my person, my soulmate, my muse, the love of my life, the father of my children, the person I will die next to.

I didn't think.
I was certain.
And he was, too.

G.59

He has:
  No education
  No job
  No car
  No money
  No real ambition
  He smokes
  He occasionally does drugs
  He doesn't work out
  He rarely brushes his teeth
  He isn't tall
  & he will be bald one day

… but my god, can he make me laugh.

G.60

In August, he came.

He bought a ticket to New York City.

We spent those ten days in love. We picked up exactly where we left off. This visit only reassured what I already knew: I loved him completely and without hesitation. He was the love of my life. These last months, trying to have a relationship over the phone was all worth it. It had amounted to something. It was all worth it. He met my family. He saw New York City, where I worked, and my life there. We fucked as if it was our sole purpose in life. We laughed together, explored the city, spent time with my mom on her farm, and delved into the U.S. culture he adored so much. What we had talked about for years finally came true; he was in America for the first time. I took this as a step in the right direction.

I told him of my plans to quit my job, travel again, and come to Australia to be with him. He needed time to think, and I respected that.

When he left to go home, I had no idea that this would be the last time I would ever see him.

I wish now I would have kissed him longer, hugged him tighter, told him how much he meant to me, how proud I was of him, confessed endlessly how much he meant to me.

A day doesn't go by without me regretting this final goodbye.

G.61

I don't know what happened.

One day, we were perfect, planning the future.
  Next, I blocked him on everything.
  We broke up.
  He doesn't know what he wants.
  I can't wait anymore.
  The only thing I can imagine is a life with him.
  Why can't he see it too?
  Doesn't he feel it too?
  Why did he come to see me if he didn't feel the same?
  Just to fuck me?
  Just to play with my heart?
  Just to torture me because he knows I won't give up on us?
  Just to feed his ego?

G.62

76 days later.

I am in the Philippines.
I unblocked him.
I missed him so much; words are not enough to describe the feeling.
Throughout the last three years, he has been my best friend, stability, and home.
I made him my everything.
He knows me better than anyone else.
I felt I needed to talk to him before I started to travel again.
That I could somehow convince him to let me come to Australia to see him.
I took 76 days to realize how much he truly meant to me.
The 76 days that passed – I didn't text, touch, flirt, or entertain any other man.
Even the idea of moving on made me physically sick to my stomach.
There was no one in the world made for me but him.
I was sure we would, once again, reunite somehow, somehow.
We would start our lives together.

G.63

In the 76 days, he told me he had met someone, that he loved her. It was later confirmed to me that in fact, he cheated on me. It wasn't even close to 76 days. To this day, it still brings me so much pain. I had been replaced. He had moved on, that we were done, that I was stupid for believing in true love, that I was living in a fairy tale. I was eating movies, that I was holding on to a love he outgrew.

Simply put, he didn't love me anymore.

He told me to stop crying and hung up the phone.

That is how I choose to remember him.
That was our last conversation.
That is how it ended.

G.64

This punctured mercilessly every atom in my body. I cried from places in my heart I didn't know I existed. Day after day, I found new depths to my sadness. I couldn't stop. I couldn't calm down. I couldn't understand. I couldn't accept it. This went on for almost four months. Reflecting back now, I see that my obsession with getting him back was not about him. It was the little girl inside me trying to prove to myself that I was worth staying for.

My world came crashing down right in front of my eyes. He moved on, while in those days, I spent every night missing him. He replaced me. He fell out of love. I could not register how I believed beyond any doubt that conclusively we were meant to be together, and he didn't feel it either.

He shattered my heart into a million fragile pieces.
   Leaving me alone to put myself back together again.
   How could the love we had evaporated so instantly?

G.65

I found myself wishing he would one day have a beautiful daughter.
One day, she would meet a man exactly like him.
They would fall madly in love.
This man would so cruelly and without any remorse break her heart, like he did mine.
Only in this moment could he finally understand what I felt.

Later, I regretted these thoughts.

I wish for him to be a better man, not the coward I know, but someone his mom, sister, and nieces would be proud of. I know one day he will. However, my deepest desire is for him to treat the women that come after with more respect and love than he gave to me.

To this day there isn't an Instagram story he doesn't view, a TikTok he doesn't watch, or a YouTube video he doesn't see.

G.66

We should have stayed strangers.

G.67

We spent the better part of three years as best friends, falling in love and traveling the world together. It was a love story even the heavens couldn't surmise. We both divested everything to make it work. We both did everything we could. There isn't a day, hour, or minute that goes by where I don't thank God for bringing him into my life, for changing my life forever. It would be a disservice to the relationship to say I loved him. It was more than that, so much more. I wanted it, more than anything, I wanted it to be him. I never imagined how much you could love a person until he came into my life. It was the hardest thing my heart has ever done to let him go, to accept that it was over. In some ways, even though we aren't meant to be together, a part of my soul feels as though it belongs to him. He did me a favor, letting me go, because I would have never given up on him and on us. He is a part of some of my most cherished memories, these memories we created together. We were just two kids, falling in love, where nothing mattered except being together. We had the world at our fingertips, just the two of us. He was my very best and dearest friend. In losing him, I lost a piece of myself. I will spend a lifetime missing him. If love were enough, we would be together right now, sitting outside, laughing together, sharing a cigarette, and drinking coffee. We'd be enjoying the morning sun, somewhere around the world, and we would be planning our future as if it were the most beautiful thing in this world.

G.68

Love is more than just a word, just a feeling.
   Love is perpetual.
   Love is a pattern of passionate devotion.
   Love doesn't start or end.
   Love is a state of being.

In collapsing our hearts,
   We both learned this.

In some ways, he will always be my soulmate.
   A part of me will always love him, a part of him will always love me,
   And this will never change.
   Now, I can look back and thank him.
   There isn't a day that passes that I am not grateful we didn't work out.
   The almost love of my life.

How To Turn a Boy Into a Man

Part Four:

Falling completely in love is entirely how you turn a boy into a man.
A boy who falls in love is never the same.
Love is the single most powerful thing in this world;
The only thing in this world that can truly transform you.
This is how you turn a boy into a man: by loving him unconditionally.

79

Timeless
Synchronicity

79.1

Too curious and illustrious to be a coincidence.
  The universe's undying crusade to compel me back to you.
  A twisted karmic bond.

The things I can never tell you are the reason for this page.

                                        The sky is the limit.

79.2

To write a whole chapter about you.
When I only thirst to articulate,
the adoration of the delicate sensitivity of the ice
in Madison Square Garden.
& the intensity of our conversations.

Thank you for all you did for me throughout the years.
Congratulations, kid.

Conclusion

The ending is never really the end.
In writing this novel, it is my way of letting go.
It's the start of a new chapter, a new book.
I will never give up on love.

To be continued…

About the Author

Somewhere - traveling, writing, and falling in love.

www.ingramcontent.com/pod-product-compliance
Lightning Source LLC
LaVergne TN
LVHW022321080426
835508LV00041B/1618